DRESDEN

Heute Today

DRESDEN

Heute   Today

Fotografie/Photographs
Jürgen Hohmuth

Text
Dieter Zumpe

Prestel
München · Berlin · London · New York

Inhalt

Contents

Blick in den Zwingerhof.
View of the Zwinger courtyard.

Kaum eine Stadt ist so wundervoll in die Landschaft eingebettet wie Dresden. Im Vogelflug von Pillnitz bis Radebeul über die Stadt zu ziehen und die Schönheit Dresdens aus dieser Perspektive zu genießen, das bietet dieses Buch. Im Zentrum der Stadt konzentrieren sich in großer Dichte Kultureinrichtungen von Weltruhm. Zwischen Semperoper und Synagoge finden sich neben der Frauenkirche und der Brühlschen Terrasse auch die Häuser der Staatlichen Kunstsammlungen Dresden. Dazu zählen der Zwinger mit Porzellansammlung und Mathematisch-Physikalischem Salon, der Semperbau mit der Gemäldegalerie Alte Meister und der Rüstkammer, das Albertinum mit Skulpturensammlung und Galerie Neuer Meister und schließlich das Dresdener Residenzschloss, das mit dem Einzug des Grünen Gewölbes und des Kupferstichkabinetts im Frühjahr 2004 seiner Vollendung als Zentrum der Staatlichen Kunstsammlungen Dresden immer näher kommt.

Die wichtigsten Kultureinrichtungen in der historischen Altstadt haben sich zusammengeschlossen: Zukünftig werden wir mit einer Stimme sprechen und die Besucher im *Kultur Quartier Dresden* herzlich begrüßen. Hier versammelt sich mit Staatsschauspiel, Semperoper und den Museen Weltkultur in selten gesehener Konzentration. Die berühmte Kulisse der Stadt, von Bernardo Bellotto auf seinen Bildern festgehalten, fügt sich bald wieder zu einem Ganzen. Die Kuppel der Frauenkirche wächst in die Höhe, im Jahre 2005 wird auch diese Lücke geschlossen sein. Auch wenn die Flut im August 2002 uns die Gefahren der Elbe vor Augen geführt hat, so lebt diese Stadt doch in Harmonie mit dem sonst so friedlichen Strom. Der Fluss verbindet die Schönheiten der Stadt und der Umgebung, vom Elbsandsteingebirge bis nach Meißen entwickelt sich eine Kulturlandschaft von atemberaubender Schönheit. Die Abbildungen dieses Bandes bieten einen neuen Blick auf Dresden, sie verstehen sich als Einladung, Dresden zu besuchen.

Dr. Martin Roth
Generaldirektor der Staatlichen
Kunstsammlungen Dresden

There are few cities that enjoy Dresden's wonderful location and this book allows us to see its attractions from a bird's-eye view from Pillnitz across the city to Radebeul. Cultural institutions of worldwide renown abound in the city centre. Located between the Semper Opera House and the Synagogue, we find, in addition to the Frauenkirche and the Brühlsche Terrasse, the museums of the Staatliche Kunstsammlungen Dresden, Dresden's State Art Collections, among them the Zwinger housing the Porcelain Collection and the Collection of Mathematical and Physical Instruments, the Gallery of Old Masters built by Gottfried Semper and the Armoury, the Albertinum with its Sculpture Collection and the Gallery of New Masters, and finally Dresden's Royal Palace that will be near completion as the heart of the State Art Collections when the Grünes Gewölbe (Green Vault) and the Prints and Drawings Collection find a new home there in spring 2004.

The most important cultural institutions in the historic Old Town have joined forces to allow them in future to speak with one voice. They certainly look forward to welcoming visitors to Dresden's "Cultural Quarter" where the state theatre, the Semper Opera House and numerous museums form a rarely seen concentration of culture. The famed view that Bernardo Bellotto captured in his paintings will soon be made whole again when the dome of the Frauenkirche, now rising ever higher, is completed in 2005 and the last gap in the cityscape is closed. Even if the floods in August 2002 made us aware of the dangers of the river Elbe, Dresden usually lives at peace with its otherwise placid river that unites the attractions of the city and the wider area. From the Elbsandsteingebirge to Meissen, it flows through breathtakingly beautiful and cultivated landscape. While this book offers us new and interesting views of the city, it is my wish that it will encourage you to visit Dresden to enjoy its treasures for yourself.

Dr. Martin Roth
Managing Director of the Dresden
State Art Collections

Dresden Heute versteht sich als aktuelle Chronik vom Zustand einer Stadt, die ihren Platz als moderne Großstadt mit hervorragenden kulturellen Traditionen in Deutschland und Europa wieder einnehmen möchte. Das einstige »Elbflorenz« existiert nur mehr in der Erinnerung. Die Nachkriegsgenerationen mühten sich, dessen Wahrzeichen aus der Trümmerwüste zu bergen und für die Nachwelt zu erhalten. Die Barockstadt an der Elbe, eingebettet in eine anmutige Fluss- und Hanglandschaft, konnte trotz Krieg und Zerstörung Vorzüge bewahren, die das einstige städtebauliche Gesamtkunstwerk noch erahnen lassen. Eine Stadt im Umbruch, die nach 1989 die Chance erhielt, vorhandene historische Bausubstanz und alte Stadtstrukturen mit moderner Architektur sinnvoll zu verbinden.

Diese Situation ist kennzeichnend für Dresden kurz vor dem 800-jährigen Stadtjubiläum 2006. Um vor der Geschichte bestehen zu können, ist die Frage angebracht, ob der Dichter Erich Kästner mit seiner Liebeserklärung an diese »wunderbare Stadt« Recht behält: »Geschichte, Kunst und Natur schweben über Stadt und Tal, vom Meißner Dom bis zum Großsedlitzer Schlosspark, wie ein von seiner eigenen Harmonie bezauberter Akkord.«

Eine Studie für die UNESCO hat zum Ziel, Stadt und Elbtal als schützenswertes Areal ins Weltkulturerbe aufzunehmen. Der Schmerz über den Verlust des alten Dresden steht nicht im Widerspruch zu der Einsicht, dass auch um Coventry, Rotterdam und Warschau getrauert wird. Symbolkraft hat ein Spruchband an der Baustelle der Frauenkirche »BRÜCKEN BAUEN – VERSÖHNUNG LEBEN«. Die internationale Diskussion zum Wiederaufbau der Quartiere am Neumarkt und darüber hinaus wird leidenschaftlich geführt. Noch ist die Vision vom schönen Dresden nicht aufgegeben, die Ausgangsbedingungen dafür sind günstiger als andernorts. Schon bald wird die Stadtsilhouette mit der im Jahr 2005 rekonstruierten Frauenkirche vollständig sein. Die Dresdener und ihre Gäste können dann den Canaletto-Blick wieder genießen.

Was sich beiderseits der Elbe, in der Neustadt oder der Südvorstadt, Blasewitz oder Hellerau, verändert hat, wird in beeindruckenden Luftbildern durch verblüffende Sichtweisen dokumentiert, so dass auch der Dresdener bisher Unbekanntes entdecken wird. Darüber hinaus wird der Blick geschärft, welche Chancen sich für eine Revitalisierung von Industriebrachen und Technikdenkmalen bieten.

Viele der Bilder wurden mit Hilfe eines unbemannten Foto-Luftschiffs aufgenommen. Der Fotograf steuert dabei die Kamera vom Boden aus über ein Monitorbild.

Der kommentierenden Auswahl historischer Ansichten steht eine Fülle von Aufnahmen gegenüber, die Dresdens Wandel faszinierend beleuchten.

Dresden Today examines the current situation of the capital of Saxony, a city keen to regain its place as a modern centre with an outstanding cultural heritage that is significant both in German and European terms. Now only memories remain of the city that before the War was known as "Florence on the Elbe". From among an expanse of rubble, post-war generations have laboured to preserve the city's landmarks for posterity. With hills to the north and south and lying within the wide basin of the River Elbe, this baroque city, despite wartime and subsequent destruction, has preserved a number of qualities that still recall the work of art that was pre-war Dresden.

Following the collapse of the G.D.R. in 1989, the city now has a chance to combine its built heritage and old urban structures with a programme of reconstruction using modern architecture. In the run-up to its 800th anniversary in 2006, it is now a place undergoing radical change. To allow us to pass muster with future generations, we might well ask ourselves whether the Dresden-born author Erich Kästner would again declare his love for this "wonderful city" as follows: "History, art and nature float over the city and valley, from the cathedral in Meissen to the palace park at Großsedlitz, like a chord enchanted by its own harmony".

A study is currently underway on behalf of UNESCO to establish that the city and the Elbe valley are worthy of conservation; ultimately the aim is to have them designated as World Heritage Sites. The pain felt at the loss of Dresden at the end of World War II has, in today's small world, given way to the realization that the loss of cities such as Coventry, Rotterdam and Warsaw was also mourned. Where Dresden's Frauenkirche is again rising into the sky, a German banner, with great symbolic power, reads: "Building bridges towards reconciliation". Debate about the reconstruction of the Neumarkt and adjacent areas is public, international and passionate. The vision of Dresden as a beautiful place has not been abandoned yet – indeed, the chances of realizing the dream are better here than elsewhere. Very soon, completion of the Frauenkirche in 2005 will restore the city's historic skyline and locals and visitors alike will then again be able to enjoy the view made famous by Canaletto.

The process of change elsewhere in the city, in the Neustadt district on the other side of the river or in more distant parts of town, is shown from unusual angles in Jürgen Hohmut's impressive aerial photographs that will offer new and surprising insights even to those born and bred in Dresden. Moreover, his photographs allow us to see where opportunity exists to make new use of derelict industrial land, disused factories or, indeed, to demolish row upon row of prefabricated housing. Many of the pictures were taken with the aid of an unmanned mini-airship, with the photographer controlling the camera from the ground via a monitor. Images of the recent floods and wartime destruction of the city are shown together with a wealth of views that examine in a fascinating way the changing face of Dresden today.

Dresden ist im Vergleich zu anderen deutschen Städten, die auf mehr als 1000 Jahre alte römische Gründungen zurückgehen, eine Stadt slawischen Ursprungs, wie der Name »Drezdany«, d.h. altsorbisch Sumpfwaldbewohner, erkennen lässt. Im Jahr 2006 feiert die Stadt ihr 800-jähriges Jubiläum; die erste Ansiedlung ist jedoch nachweislich älter. Um die Wende vom 6. zum 7. Jahrhundert ließen sich die Slawen im Elbtal nieder.

Im Verlauf der christlichen Missionierung, die von der Mark Meißen ausging, entstand an dem für den Handel wichtigen Flussübergang eine Kaufmannssiedlung. Die Wiege Sachsens war die Burg des Markgrafen von Meißen und der dazugehörige Bischofssitz. Wachsen und Werden der später nach Dresden verlegten Residenz sind eng mit den Wettinern verknüpft, die als eines der ältesten deutschen Fürstenhäuser über 800 Jahre auch die Geschicke Dresdens mitbestimmten.

Markgraf Heinrich der Erlauchte trug im 13. Jahrhundert wesentlich zum Ausbau Dresdens bei, indem er die Stadt mit umfangreichen Privilegien ausstattete. Zudem stiftete er das Maternihospital neben der Frauenkirche und erhob die Nicolaikirche, eine alte Kaufmannskirche, durch Schenkung einer Reliquie in den Rang einer Wallfahrtskirche.

Um 1300 wird mit der Kreuzkirche am Altmarkt auch die städtische Lateinschule erwähnt, die zugleich Chorknaben ausbildete. Wiederholt wurde die Stadtentwicklung durch verheerende Hochwasserkatastrophen wie 1342, die Pest sowie durch Brandkatastrophen unterbrochen.

Unter Markgraf Wilhelm I. (dem Einäugigen) erfolgte nicht nur der weitere Ausbau der Burg als zweite Wohnresidenz, sondern auch die Verleihung des Stadtrechts an die vis à vis gelegene Siedlung Altendresden, in der ein Augustinerkloster gegründet wurde. Zugleich brach der tatkräftige Landesherr die Macht der Burggrafen von Dohna und sicherte dadurch die Handelswege von Dresden nach Böhmen. Zu seinen Verdiensten gehörte auch der Neubau der Kreuzkirche, die 1388 geweiht wurde.

Als Schutzmaßnahme vor den aus Böhmen einfallenden Hussiten verstärkte der Dresdener Rat die Stadtbefestigung durch den Bau eines zweiten Mauerrings, dennoch konnte die Einnahme von Altendresden nicht verhindert werden. Nur wenige Steinbauten wie Kirchen und das Rathaus bestimmten damals das Stadtbild, mit Holzschindeln gedeckte Fachwerkhäuser aus Lehm dominierten.

Ende des 14. Jahrhunderts lebten knapp 4000 Einwohner (mit den Vorstädten und Altendresden ca. 5000) in Dresden, eine bescheidene Zahl, die auch im 15. Jahrhundert stagnierte. 1485, nach der Leipziger Teilung des wettinischen Besitzes, gaben die beiden Brüder Ernst und Albrecht Meißen endgültig auf und wählten Dresden zur Residenzstadt, in der fortan die Herzöge und Kurfürsten aus der Linie der Albertiner regierten. Nachdem 1491 die Stadt durch einen verheerenden Brand in Schutt und Asche gelegt worden war, erließ der Herzog eine Bauordnung, die eine Ausführung der städtischen Häuser zumindest bis in den ersten Stock in Stein und die Dachdeckung durch Ziegel vorsah.

Eine umfangreiche Bautätigkeit – gefördert durch den Hof – setzte ein, die mit dem Neubau der Kreuzkirche und dem Georgenbau im Schloss einherging, so dass im 16. Jahrhundert eine ansehnliche Renaissancestadt entstand. Dennoch hatten andere sächsische Städte wie Freiberg, Annaberg und Leipzig weit mehr Einwohner als Dresden. Herzog Georg sperrte sich gegen die Einführung der Reformation. Bis zu seinem Tode 1539 blieb er ein

Compared with other German cities whose origins as Roman foundations go back more than 1,000 years, Dreden is of Slav origin, as the name "Drezdany" suggests – Old Sorbian, meaning "inhabitant of marshy forest". In 2006, the city will celebrate its 800th anniversary, although the original settlement is known to be older. Slavs settled in the River Elbe valley at the turn of the sixth to the seventh century.

In the course of Christianisation, which started in the Meissen marches, a settlement was established at an important river crossing used by traders. The birthplace of Saxony was the castle of the Margrave of Meissen and its bishopric. The growth of the royal capital that was later transferred to Dresden is closely associated with the house of Wettin, one of Germany's oldest royal houses. It influenced Dresden's fortunes for over 800 years.

Margrave Henry the Illustrious made a vital contribution to the growth of the city in the thirteenth century by conferring on it extensive privileges. He founded the Maternihospital beside the Frauenkirche and, by donating a relic, elevated the Nicolaikirche (church of St. Nicholas), the old church of the merchant classes, to the rank of a pilgrimage church.

Around 1300, documents mention the Kreuzkirche on Altmarkt and the town's grammar school, which also trained choristers. Devastating floods, such as in 1342, the plague and major fires repeatedly interrupted the growth of the town.

Under Margrave William I (the One-Eyed), the castle was further developed as the second royal residence, and Altendresden, on the other side of the river, was granted a town charter and an Augustinian monastery was founded there. At the same time, he destroyed the power of the burgraves of Dohna, thus securing the trade routes from Dresden to Bohemia. It is also thanks to William I that the Kreuzkirche was re-built and consecrated in 1388.

To offer protection against the Hussites on their incursions from Bohemia, Dresden's city fathers upgraded the city's fortifications with the construction of a second ring wall, although the improvements failed to prevent the district of Altendresden from being taken. Only a few stone

Der »Fürstenzug« an der Augustusstraße. 1907 wurde die Sgraffito-Malerei durch Porzellankacheln ersetzt. Abgebildet sind sämtliche sächsischen Fürsten und Könige sowie die Vertreter der verschiedenen Stände.
The "Procession of Princes" depicts all of Saxony's kings and princes followed by representatives of the various classes. In 1907, the original sgraffito work was replaced by porcelain tiles.

erbitterter Gegner der Lehren Martin Luthers, erst danach ging das Land vom katholischen zum evangelischen Glauben über. Unter dem ehrgeizigen Herzog und späteren Kurfürsten Moritz wurde der Baumeister Caspar Voigt von Wierandt beauftragt, die Stadtbefestigung in westlicher Richtung und bis zur Elbe zu erweitern. In der Folgezeit vollendete Kurfürst August, der seinem Bruder Moritz nach dessen frühem Tod 1553 nachfolgte, das umfangreiche Befestigungswerk nach italienisch-niederländischem Vorbild. Mit der Regierungszeit beider Kurfürsten (August regierte bis 1586) ist der wirtschaftliche und politische Aufschwung des kursächsischen Staates verbunden, der sich auch städtebaulich günstig auswirkte. Baumeister wie Paul Buchner, dem das Zeughaus (an gleicher Stelle steht das heutige Albertinum) zu verdanken ist, Rochus von Lynar, der Italiener Giovanni Maria Nosseni und die Bildhauerfamilie Walther prägten das Baugeschehen. Erstmals brachten die italienischen Brüder Thola die Sgraffito-Malerei nach Dresden. Die erste Vierflügel-Schlossanlage der Renaissance in Deutschland entstand. Diese Zeugnisse wie auch Reste des ehemaligen Jägerhofes (heute Museum für Volkskunst) auf der Neustädte Seite sind noch erhalten bzw. wurden rekonstruiert. Unmittelbar am Schloss erbaute Hans Irmisch das Kanzleihaus, das älteste Verwaltungsgebäude der Stadt. Neue Kirchenbauten und das Erhöhen vorhandener Türme sowie der 1557 erfolgte Neubau der Kreuzschule vollzogen den Wandel Dresdens von einer bescheidenen Ackerbürgerstadt zur dicht bebauten Handwerker- und Handelsstadt mit repräsentativen Bauten und gepflasterten Straßen.

Der wirtschaftlich weitblickend handelnde Kurfürst August gründete nicht nur die einzige Münzstätte im Lande, sondern auch das Kammergut Ostra als landwirtschaftlichen Musterbetrieb. Gleichzeitig erweiterte »Vater August« die von seinem Bruder eingerichtete Kantorei unter Johann Walther zur Hofkapelle mit 45 Mitgliedern. Besondere Verdienste, von denen wir noch heute profitieren, erwarb sich August mit dem Einrichten der Kunstkammer, der ersten großen wissenschaftlich-technischen Sammlung in Europa, die zusammen mit einer Bücherei den Grundstock für die berühmten Staatlichen Kunstsammlungen bildete.

Das 17. Jahrhundert brachte mit dem Dreißigjährigen Krieg (1618–1648) eine Dezimierung der Bevölkerung mit sich; mehrmals wütete die Pest, Plünderungen und Kriegslasten führten zu Armut. Das Gewerbe stagnierte, obwohl zahlreiche Exulanten nach Dresden kamen. Herausragend in diesen Notzeiten war die Musikpflege, die von dem »Vater der deutschen Musik« Heinrich Schütz, seit 1615 für 57 Jahre Kapellmeister der Hofkapelle, getragen wurde, ergänzt durch die städtischen Kreuzkantoren.

Die Glanzzeit Dresdens ist eng an das Augusteische Zeitalter gebunden, das die absolutistische Regierung von August II. (August der Starke) und seinem Sohn August III. von 1697 bis 1763 umfasste. Durch den Erwerb der polnischen Königskrone entstand eine Situation, die dem Ausbau zur Metropole der kurzzeitig existierenden polnisch-sächsischen Union entgegenkam. Der Kurfürst-König bediente durch eigene Entwürfe und das ihm unterstellte Oberlandbauamt, das auch die städtischen Planungen kontrollierte – wie beim Bau der Frauenkirche von George Bähr – seinen Ehrgeiz, den Aufstieg Dresdens zur europäischen Residenz von Rang zu forcieren. Die hervorragende Anbindung von Schlössern (Pillnitz, Japanisches Palais, Übigau) und später der Hofkirche von Gaetano Chiaveri an die Elbe in Anlehnung an den venezianischen Canal Grande, lassen die barocke

buildings, such as churches and the town hall, lent the townscape its character around this time; half-timbered buildings of wooden shingles and mortar predominated.

In the late fourteenth century, Dresden had just under 4,000 inhabitants (5,000 including the suburbs and Altendresden); this was a modest number that remained static during the fifteenth century. In 1485, following Leipzig's partition of Wettin possessions, the two brothers Ernst and Albrecht finally relinquished Meissen, and chose Dresden instead as the seat of their court. It was from there that the dukes and electors of the Albertine line henceforth ruled. In 1491, the town was reduced to ashes by a huge fire, thus prompting the duke to introduce building regulations that required homes to be built of stone and to be roofed with tiles. An extensive building programme began – encouraged by the court – that coincided with the reconstruction of the Kreuzkirche and the Georgenbau within the palace.

During the sixteenth century, Dresden thus grew into a town with handsome Renaissance buildings. Nevertheless, Freiberg, Annaberg and Leipzig still had many more inhabitants than Dresden. Duke Georg resisted the introduction of the Reformation. Up until his death in 1539 he remained a bitter opponent of the teachings of Martin Luther. Only after it did Dresden convert to the Protestant faith. Under the ambitious Duke Moritz, the architect Caspar Voigt von Wierandt was commissioned to extend the city's defences westwards and towards the river. The Elector August, who succeeded his brother Moritz on his premature death in 1553, subsequently completed the city's extensive fortifications along Italian and Dutch lines. The reign of both these Electors (August reigned until 1586) is associated with the economic and political ascent of the Electorate of Saxony that in turn boosted urban development. Master builders like Paul Buchner, to whom we owe the Zeughaus (where the Albertinum now stands), Rochus von Lynar, the Italian Giovanni Maria Nosseni and the Walther family of sculptors had a decisive influence on building activity. The Italian Thola brothers introduced sgraffito technique to Dresden. The German Renaissance's first palace boasting two sets of wings was built.

Bernardo Bellotto, *Dresden vom rechten Elbufer unterhalb der Augustusbrücke*, 1748.
Bernardo Bellotto, *Dresden Seen from the Right Bank of the Elbe River*, 1748.

Meisterschaft auch heute noch erkennen. Die Festkultur nahm ungeahnte Ausmaße an. August der Starke inszenierte sich bei prunkvollen Aufzügen und bediente sich hierbei des Erfindungsreichtums seiner Baumeister und Künstler. Anlässlich der Vermählungsfeierlichkeiten seines Sohnes 1719 dauerten die Festlichkeiten mehrere Wochen: Maskeraden und Karussells im Zwinger, Regatten und Feuerwerke auf der Elbe sowie Opernaufführungen wechselten sich ab.

Manufakturen für die Herstellung von Luxusgegenständen entstanden. Nach der Erfindung des europäischen Hartporzellans 1709 stellte der König die Porzellanmanufaktur unter seine Aufsicht. Der Zwinger von Matthäus Daniel Pöppelmann und dem Bildhauer Balthasar Permoser, Schloss Pillnitz, das Residenzschloss und das benachbarte Taschenbergpalais sowie die Frauenkirche und die Hofkirche sind längst zu Wahrzeichen der Stadt geworden. Ein ganzer Stab von Gouverneuren, Architekten und Baumeistern wie Johann Christoph Knöffel, Jean de Bodt, Zacharias Longuelune u.a. baute Adelspaläste, die den höfischen Bauten in nichts nachstanden. In den berühmten Veduten des Hofmalers Bernardo Bellotto, genannt Canaletto, sind sie verewigt. Mit der Niederlegung der Festungswerke infolge der regen Bautätigkeit erweiterte sich die Stadtfläche von Dresden, so dass um 1755 ca. 63 000 Einwohner gezählt wurden.

Der Siebenjährige Krieg (1756–1763), den Preußen Sachsen aufzwang, zerrüttete Wirtschaft und Staat. Durch Artilleriebeschuss war etwa die Hälfte der Altstadt zerstört. Nur langsam erholten sich Stadt und Land. Wenige Neubauten wie das Landhaus (heute Stadtmuseum) und das Gewandhaus (heute Hotel) entstanden. Wegen ihrer schmucklosen Fassaden galten die meisten Gebäude als Zeugnisse für den »Dresdener Hungerstil«.

Mit der Besetzung Dresdens durch die Franzosen, Sachsen war 1806 dem Rheinbund beigetreten, herrschte ab 1813 unvorstellbares Elend. Sachsen war ein besiegtes Land.

Der endgültige Abbruch des Festungsgürtels nach Napoleons Vertreibung ermöglichte die Öffnung der Stadt zur malerischen Landschaft. Die bereits vom Premierminister Brühl unter August III. angelegte Brühlsche Terrasse wurde durch eine Freitreppe zugänglich und als »Balkon Europas« zur Flaniermeile. Statt der hohen Bürgerhäuser mit Barockfassaden und den typischen steilen Mansardendächern dominierten einfache kubische Haustypen mit Satteldächern, die man als »Kaffeemühlen« verspottete. Nach dem Wiener Kongress von 1815 verlor Sachsen die Hälfte seines Territoriums an Preußen. Erst mit der sprunghaften Industrialisierung und dem damit verbunden Ausbau der Eisenbahnlinien und Bahnhöfe im Stadtgebiet legte Dresden die sichtbare Armut ab. Den Nachfolgern Friedrich August des Gerechten, der ein Vertreter der Restauration war, blieb es vorbehalten, der Residenz ein neues Antlitz zu geben.

Mit Gottfried Semper kam ein Baukünstler in die Stadt, dessen Leitstil die italienische Hochrenaissance war und der nicht nur in Dresden die Architektur nachhaltig prägte. Der Theaterplatz mit der den Zwinger abschließenden Gemäldegalerie und das königliche Hoftheater – die heutige Semperoper – sind sein Werk. Sein Baustil erwies sich als Initialzündung für nachfolgende Bauwerke wie die drei Elbschlösser oder die großzügige Villenarchitektur des 19. Jahrhunderts, die den Wohlstand Großindustrieller und Pensionäre widerspiegelten.

These and the remains of the former Jägerhof (hunting lodge; now the Museum of Folk Art) in the Neustadt district across the river are still standing or have been rebuilt. Immediately beside the palace, Hans Irmisch built the chancellery, the city's oldest administrative centre. New churches, work to heighten towers and the construction in 1557 of the Kreuzschule (school) completed Dresden's transformation from a modest town of smallholders to a densely populated centre of trade and manufacture with representative buildings and cobbled streets.

The Elector Augustus was a prudent man who promoted the economy. He founded not only Saxony's sole mint, but also developed the crown land at Ostra as a model agricultural business. At the same time, "Father Augustus" expanded to 45 members the choir and instrumental ensemble that his brother had established and placed them in the charge of Johan Walther. Augustus made a hugely valuable contribution that benefits us to this day when he established the Kunstkammer, the first major scientific collection in Europe; together with a library, it formed the basis of Dresden's renowned Staatliche Kunstsammlungen (State Art Collections).

The Thirty Years' War (1618–48) ravaged the population: the plague struck several times; looting and the burdens of war led to poverty. Business stagnated although Protestant refugees from the Hapsburg monarchy settled in Dresden where, in a time of general hardship, the cultivation of music was a salient feature. Heinrich Schütz, the "father of German music", took up the post of chapel master in the electoral chapel in 1615 and held it for 57 years.

Dresden's golden age and the reign of the absolute monarch Augustus II (Augustus the Strong) and that of his son, Augustus III, from 1697 to 1763, are inextricably linked. When the electors of Saxony also became the kings of Poland, they were able to develop the city as the capital of the short-lived union between Saxony and Poland. Using his own plans, and the building control office that examined town planning proposals (as in the case of George Bähr's Frauenkirche), and which was also answerable to him, the Elector-King was able to satisfy his ambition of seeing Dresden rise to the first rank of European royal capitals. Taking Venice's Canale Grande as a model, the palaces (Pillnitz, Japanese, Übigau) and, later on, Gaetano Chiaveri's Hofkirche, were set in marvellous relation to the Elbe and remain to this day examples of Baroque virtuosity. His celebratory lifestyle acquired hitherto unknown dimensions: in splendid processions, Augustus the Strong made himself the star attraction by exploiting the capacity for invention of his master builders and artists. Celebrations marking the marriage of his son in 1719 lasted several weeks: masquerades and tournaments were held in the Zwinger, regattas and firework displays were staged on the Elbe and one opera performance followed another.

Workshops were opened to produce luxury goods. Following the invention of European hard-fired porcelain in 1709, the king placed its manufacture under his control. The Zwinger, built by Matthäus Daniel Pöppelmann and the sculptor Balthasar Permoser, Pillnitz Palace, the Royal Palace and the neighbouring Taschenberg Palace as well as the Frauenkirche and the Hofkirche have long been symbols of the city. Numerous governors, architects and master builders including Johann Christoph Knöffel, Jean de Bodt and Zacharias Longuelune, built palaces for the aristocracy that were the equal of anything the King had. Indeed, they are immortalised in the famous

Nach dem Deutsch-Französischen Krieg 1870/71 wurden die städtebaulichen Proportionen zum Teil gesprengt. Die überdimensionierten Ministerialbauten am Neustädter Ufer, die Kunstakademie sowie der Kuppelbau des Sächsischen Kunstvereins an der Brühlschen Terrasse sind Beleg dafür. Fast explosionsartig vollzog sich in den letzten Jahrzehnten des 19. Jahrhunderts der Übergang zur Großstadt mit mehr als 100 000 Einwohnern. Am 9. November 1918 dankte der letzte sächsische König Friedrich August III. ab. Dresden, nunmehr Verwaltungszentrum des Freistaates Sachsen, war keine Residenzstadt mehr. Durch Eingemeindung der Garnison, die in der Albertstadt entstanden war, und anderer Vorstädte und Dörfer expandierte die Stadt, so dass Dresden vor dem Zweiten Weltkrieg zu den fünf größten Städten Deutschlands gehörte. Trotz der Zunahme an Industrie, die in den Randgebieten siedelte, blieb Dresden eine elegante Verwaltungs-, Kunst- und Hochschulstadt mit einem überwiegend barocken Altstadtzentrum, das sich im Glanz der Vergangenheit sonnte und jährlich Hunderttausende Touristen anzog. Bereits vor dem Ersten Weltkrieg wurden vom Stadtbaurat Hans Erlwein Versuche unternommen, den konservativen Baustil aufzulockern. Zweckbauten wie der Schlachthof und der später nach ihm benannte Speicher, aber auch Schulen und eine Feuerwache sowie das Italienische Dörfchen am Elbkai blieben erhalten. Als geradezu revolutionär erwies sich das Konzept der im Norden der Stadt gelegenen Gartenstadt Hellerau, das von englischen Lebensreformideen beeinflusst war. Dort entstanden neben beispielhaften Siedlungen für die Arbeiter der Deutschen Werkstätten auch wegweisende Bauten der Moderne wie das Festspielhaus von Heinrich Tessenow. Beim später entstandenen Deutschen Hygienemuseum von Wilhelm Kreis bleibt der Anklang zur monumentalen Staatsarchitektur der Nationalsozialisten unübersehbar.

Als einzige deutsche Großstadt blieb »Elbflorenz« bis Anfang 1945 unversehrt. Am 13. und 14. Februar flogen die Bomberflotten der Alliierten schwere Luftangriffe. Der Feuersturm vernichtete die Innenstadt auf einem

Blick vom Rathausturm auf die zerstörte Innenstadt.
The centre of Dresden in ruins, view from the town hall tower.

views of the city by the court painter Bernardo Bellotto, better known as Canaletto. As a result of the great increase in building activity, the city's fortifications were razed. Dresden's area expanded and in 1755 the city had about 63,000 inhabitants.

The Seven Years' War (1756–63), waged on Saxony by Prussia, ruined the economy and the state. Artillery fire destroyed around half of the old town, and the city and state recovered only slowly. Only a few buildings were constructed, among them the Landhaus (now a local history museum) and the Gewandhaus (cloth merchants' hall, now a hotel). Because of their plain frontages, most buildings were said to be representative of Dresden's "lean style".

With the French occupation of Dresden (Saxony had joined the League of the Rhine in 1806), there was unimaginable misery in the city from 1813 on. Saxony had been well and truly defeated.

Following Napoleon's expulsion, the complete removal of its defensive ring allowed the city to open out to its picturesque surroundings. The Brühlsche Terrasse had already been laid out by the prime minister under Augustus III, Brühl; a flight of stairs was built to give access to it and, known as the Balcony of Europe, it became *the* place to promenade in. The tall houses with their baroque façades and steep mansard roofs that were typical for the wealthy middle classes were replaced by simple, cube-shaped houses with gable roofs that were scathingly referred to as "coffee grinders". Following the Congress of Vienna (1815), Saxony lost half of its territory to Prussia. Not until the period of rapid industrialisation, associated with the growth of the railways and the construction of stations within the city, did Dresden shed its air of visible poverty. It fell to the successors of Frederick Augustus the Just, a supporter of the Restoration, to give new form to the Residence.

Enter the architect Gottfried Semper, a man who embraced the Cinquecento Revival and who had a lasting influence not only on the architecture of Dresden. The Theaterplatz (Theatre Square) and the Gemäldegalerie (art gallery) that completes the Zwinger and the royal court theatre – known now as the Semperoper – are his work. His style showed the way ahead for later buildings that expressed the wealth acquired by industrialists and retired officials. It is reflected in nineteenth-century villa architecture, and most especially in the three palaces on the banks of the Elbe.

After the Franco-German war of 1870–71, architectural proportions expanded hugely, as is seen in the vast size of the government buildings on Neustädter Ufer, the art academy and the domed building housing the Saxon Society for the Promotion of Fine Arts (Kunstverein) on Brühlsche Terrasse. In the last decades of the nineteenth century, the city underwent rapid change, and its population increased to over 100,000. The last king of Saxony, Frederick Augustus III, abdicated on 9 November 1918, and Dresden ceased to be a royal capital; instead it became the administrative centre of the Free State of Saxony. By incorporating the garrison in Albertstadt district, as well as other suburbs and villages, Dresden grew to such an extent that it was one of Germany's five largest cities just before World War II. Despite the growth of industry along its periphery, Dresden remained an elegant centre of administration, the arts and tertiary education with a largely baroque Old Town in whose faded glory its citizens basked and which attracted hundreds of thousands of visitors annually. Even before

Gebiet von 15 Quadratkilometern und kostete einer bis heute nicht genau bekannten Zahl von Opfern das Leben. Dresden, die weltberühmte Kunstmetropole mit großer Tradition, sollte nach dem Krieg unter dem Einfluss der sowjetischen Besatzungsmacht und der von ihr eingesetzten SED-Stadtverwaltung als »sozialistische Großstadt« neu entstehen. Dennoch war die Erinnerung an das alte Dresden so stark, dass einige der bis auf die Grundmauern zerstörten Gebäude in den ersten Nachkriegsjahren gesichert und später wieder aufgebaut wurden. Andere, wie die gotische Sophienkirche oder ganze Straßenzüge um den Neumarkt, wurden bis Anfang der sechziger Jahre rücksichtslos abgerissen, um Platz für ein Zentrum mit übergroßen Aufmarschflächen zu schaffen. Das Vorgehen versierter Kommunalpolitiker und Denkmalschützer verhinderte Schlimmeres. Trotzdem ließ sich das Wuchern des Wohnungsbaus in Gestalt monotoner Plattenbauten bis ins Stadtzentrum hinein nicht aufhalten.

Die Wende 1989 stoppte die »zweite Zerstörung« Dresdens, die mit dem Verfall von Altbausubstanz einherging. Auf der Grundlage eines west-östlichen Architekturworkshops wurde ein Stadtleitbild erstellt, das den alten Grundriss in der Mitte der Stadt teilweise wieder aufnahm. Der durch eine weltweite Bürgerinitiative zustande gekommene Wiederaufbau der Frauenkirche als Mahnmal der Versöhnung und der Neubau der Synagoge haben Signalwirkung. Richtungsweisend für die weitere Stadtgestaltung sind Beispiele moderner Architektur wie der Landtag von Peter Kulka sowie die Sanierung historischer Bausubstanz.

Die Wiedergewinnung des historischen Neumarkts lässt hoffen, das Dresden seine Mitte und damit seine Seele wiederfindet, die in den Bewohnern und nicht den Sandsteinen zuhause ist. Lücken im historischen Stadtbild können geschlossen werden, aber lebendig bleibt die Stadt nur durch eine den Anforderungen an eine moderne Großstadt angepasste Architektur. Goethes Worte am Schauspielhaus könnten dafür programmatisch sein: »Ältestes bewahrt mit Treue – freundlich aufgefasstes Neue«.

World War I, the city architect, Hans Erlwein, tried to moderate the city's conservative style of architecture. Functional buildings like the slaughterhouse and warehouses, schools and a fire station have remained intact, as has the Italian Village in Theaterplatz. Nothing short of revolutionary, the garden village of Hellerau was laid out in the north of the city, its design influenced by ideas from England. A number of early modern classics were also built, among them Tessenow's theatre. Wilhelm Kreis's Deutsches Hygienemuseum, built later, is unmistakably reminiscent of the monumental style favoured by the Nazis.

Until the beginning of 1945, Dresden was the only major German city that had not been bombed. During the night of 13–14 February, British and American aircraft attacked in force: eight square miles of the city centre were devastated in a firestorm.

Under the influence of the Soviet occupying power, and the Socialist Unity Party of Germany that it installed in the city's administration, Dresden, with its long tradition as a world-famous centre of art, was to be rebuilt as a "socialist city". Yet memories of old Dresden were so potent that the Zwinger was rebuilt during the immediate post-war era followed by the opera house in 1985. Salvageable ruins, such as the Gothic Sophienkirche, and burned-out streets were ruthlessly demolished by the start of the 1960s to make way for a centre capable of staging huge marches. Worse was prevented from happening by the action of experienced people in local politics and other campaigners. Nevertheless, monotonous prefabs could not be prevented from encroaching into the very heart of the city.

The "second destruction" of Dresden, accompanied by widespread decay of the city's buildings, came to an end with the political events of 1989. Experts from the east and west have since then developed a blueprint for the city that partly adopts the old street plan in the city centre. Thanks to campaigners with supporters around the world, the Frauenkirche is now being reconstructed as a monument to reconciliation. Both it and the city's new synagogue have an important function as symbols.

Peter Kulka's Landtag (Saxon parliament) and the refurbishment of old tenements are two examples of successful contemporary architecture at work in the city.

It is to be hoped that the restoration of the historic Neumarkt along old building lines will allow Dresden to regain its centre and its soul, which resides in its citizens, not in the sandstone round about them. Wounds can be healed, but currently the city needs to be rejuvenated using liveable buildings. We could well heed Goethe's words inscribed on the city's theatre: "Faithfully preserve the old and welcome in the new."

Der Wiederaufbau der Grunaer Straße im Stadtzentrum, um 1951.
The reconstructed Grunaer Strasse in the city centre, around 1951.

Zwinger und Gemäldegalerie

Der Zwinger, am 13. Februar 1945 zerstört und nach dem Krieg wieder-aufgebaut, steht als Symbol für den Überlebenswillen der Stadt und ihrer Bewohner. Zunächst als Festplatz konzipiert und anlässlich des Besuchs des Dänenkönigs 1709 als hölzerne Festarchitektur gezimmert, entwarf Matthäus Daniel Pöppelmann 1710 nach einer Ideenskizze seines könig-lichen Bauherren eine Orangerie aus Sandstein. Die anschließenden Längs-galerien, bestückt mit vier Pavillons an den Ecken, bilden einen annähernd quadratischen Innenhof, der an den Langseiten durch kleinere Seitenhöfe erweitert wird. Als bedeutendstes Werk Pöppelmanns gilt der 1716 entstan-dene Wallpavillon, der von der sechs Meter hohen Figur des *Hercules Saxo-nicus* bekrönt ist. Eine der vielen Schöpfungen des Bildhauers Balthasar Permoser. Das Kronentor ragt mit seiner zwiebelförmig geschwungenen Dachhaube gleich einem römischen Triumphbogen aus der Langgalerie am Zwingergraben heraus. Vier vergoldete polnische Adler und die Königskrone bilden den Abschluss. Die symmetrisch angelegten Becken der Spring-brunnen unterstreichen das heitere Spiel zwischen Natur und Architektur, gerahmt von einer barocken Säulen- und Pilasterarchitektur und noch ein-mal gesteigert im außerhalb des Zwingerhofs gelegenen Nymphenbad – ein Festsaal unter freien Himmel, wie ihn die Italiener kennen. Die im Stil der italienischen Hochrenaissance errichtete Gemäldegalerie begrenzt seit 1855 den bis dahin offenen Zwinger. »Die sämtlichen Gebäude sind durch eine rings herum geführte Galerie miteinander vereinigt, es pflegen ... viele Einwohner der Stadt spazieren zugehen, welche sich an den lustigen Aus-sichten ... daselbst ergötzen«, so der Architekt über den Nutzen seines Bauwerks, das heute die Schätze der Staatlichen Kunstsammlungen (u.a. die Gemäldegalerie Alte Meister sowie die neugestaltete Porzellangalerie) wie in einer kostbaren Vitrine präsentiert.

Zwinger and Art Gallery

The Zwinger, meaning outer bailey, was destroyed in the bombing raid of the night of 13–14 February 1945. The rebuilt complex is testimony to the determination of the citizens of Dresden never to relinquish the sparkling creations of Dresden Baroque. Designed initially as a venue for festivities, and cobbled together in wood for the visit of the king of Denmark, the Zwinger was later built in sandstone as an orangery, its architect Matthäus Daniel Pöppelmann working to drawings made by the King. The adjoining Längsgalerien (Long Galleries), with four pavilions in each corner, form an almost square courtyard that has smaller courtyards off along its sides. The Wallpavillon (Rampart Pavilion) of 1716, surmounted by the six-metre-tall figure of Hercules Saxonicus, is regarded as one of Pöppelmann's most significant designs; it is the work of Balthasar Permoser. Rising in the centre of the Langgalerie (Long Gallery) parallel to the moat and resembling a Roman triumphal arch is the lavishly decorated, onion-shaped Kronentor (Crown Gate) surmounted by the crown and Polish and imperial eagles resplendent in gold leaf. The basins surrounding the fountains are arranged symmetrically, and accentuate the joyful interplay between architecture and water. They are enclosed by baroque columns and pilasters whose effect is further intensified by the surrounding Nymphs' Bath – a room open to the sky, such as is found in Italy. The Gemäldegalerie, in the style of the Italian High Renaissance, opened in 1855; until it was built, the Zwinger had been open to the river. "All the buildings are connected by a gallery. Many resi-dents promenade there and take great pleasure in the delightful views", according to the architect's description of the usefulness of his building that today houses the Staatliche Kunstsammlungen (State Art Collections), including the refurbished Porcelain Collection and the Gemäldegalerie Alte Meister.

Glockenspielpavillon mit abendlicher Beleuchtung.
The carillon pavilion in the evening light.

Der überflutete Zwingerhof am 18. August 2002.
18 August 2002: the courtyard of the Zwinger Palace under water.

Blick über den Zwingerhof nach Norden.
View of the Zwinger courtyard facing north.

Theaterplatz

Theaterplatz

Die Pläne von Matthäus Daniel Pöppelmann für eine Erweiterung des Zwingers bis zur Elbe vom Anfang des 18. Jahrhunderts nahm Gottfried Semper wieder auf, indem er mit dem Bau des neuen Hoftheaters 1838/41 seinen eigenen Forumsplan im Ansatz verwirklichte. Flankiert von der Gemäldegalerie, ebenfalls von Semper entworfen, aber von Karl Moritz Haenel ausgeführt, ergänzt die Anlage einen der schönsten Plätze der Welt. Die baukünstlerischen Leistungen bedeutender Architekten verschiedener Epochen sind hier weiträumig versammelt und mit ihren Sichtachsen auf das Reiterdenkmal von König Johann ausgerichtet, ein Werk von Johannes Schilling, das erst 1883 hinzukam. Den äußeren Rahmen des Theaterplatzes schaffen die Kathedrale St. Trinitatis (ehemalige Katholische Hofkirche), der Westflügel des Schlosses und die vorgelagerte Altstädter Wache – nach einem Entwurf Karl Friedrich Schinkels, eines der wenigen Beispiele für den Klassizismus in Dresden. Den Abschluss zur Elbseite bildet das von Hans Erlwein errichtete »Italienische Dörfchen« von 1911/13. Der Name des Restaurants stammt von den Arbeits- und Wohnquartieren italienischer Gastarbeiter, die am Bau der Hofkirche beschäftigt waren. Etwas versteckt in der Nische zwischen Gemäldegalerie und Zwingerwall, dafür romantisch verträumt, steht das Denkmal des Komponisten Carl Maria von Weber, eine Schöpfung des Dresdener Bildhauers Ernst Rietschel. Wie die für sich einzigartigen Gebäude miteinander korrespondieren, muss man an Ort und Stelle erleben. Erlwein zitiert am Eingangsbereich zum »Italienischen Dörfchen« Stilelemente wie die ionischen Säulen, die sich an der Schinkelwache wiederfinden. Dieser zu jeder Tageszeit von Menschen belebte Platz lässt mediterranes Lebensgefühl aufkommen und vergessen, das alle diese Gebäude 1945 zerstört waren.

When, from 1838–41, Gottfried Semper built the new Hoftheater (court theatre), to some extent he realised Pöppelmann's ambitious eighteenth-century plan for a square. Rounding off one of the world's most handsome squares, the theatre stands a short distance from the Gemäldegalerie (art gallery), again designed by Semper but carried out by Karl Moritz Haenel. In the Theaterplatz are amassed the achievements of great architects from different eras, their sight lines orientated towards Johannes Schilling's equestrian statue of King Johann that was erected only in 1883. The Theaterplatz is also flanked by St. Trinitatis cathedral (formerly the Catholic court church), the west wing of the Schloss (royal palace), Schinkel's Altstädter Wache (guardhouse), one of the rare examples of Classicism in Dresden, and, on the riverside, the Italienisches Dörfchen (Italian Village), built from 1911–13 to a design by Hans Erlwein. The name of the inn, Italienisches Dörfchen, reminds us that this is where the Italian craftsmen who worked on the Hofkirche once lived. At its entrance, Erlwein makes use of Ionic columns such as are also found on Schinkel's guardhouse and Greek temples. Between the art gallery and the wall around the Zwinger, somewhat out of the way but all the more romantic and idyllic for it, is a memorial to the composer Carl Maria von Weber; it is the work of local sculptor Ernst Rietschel, a notable representative of the Dresden school. How each of these unique buildings relates to each other, despite the distances between them, is best experienced on the spot. Crowded with people throughout the day, this square creates a feeling of Mediterranean warmth and enables one to forget that all its buildings were destroyed in 1945.

Blick elbaufwärts über den Theaterplatz mit Hofkirche, Semperoper und Italienischem Dörfchen.
Looking upriver across Theaterplatz with the Hofkirche, the Semper Opera House and the Italian Village.

Kathedrale und Schloss bilden wieder ein geschlossenes Ensemble.
The cathedral and the Royal Palace once again form a unified whole.

Semperoper

Semper Opera House

Dresden ist ohne die Oper nicht denkbar. In Schlossnähe stand als erster Vorgängerbau der heutigen Institution seit 1667 das »Churfürstliche Opernhaus am Taschenberg«. 1719 lässt August der Starke anlässlich der Vermählungsfeierlichkeiten für seinen Sohn das Große Opernhaus am Zwinger von italienischen Baumeistern unter Mitwirkung Pöppelmanns errichten. Es wird zum Zentrum barocker Opernkultur in Deutschland. Johann Adolf Hasse (»der göttliche Sachse«) sowie Johann Gottlieb Naumann leiten eine glanzvolle Epoche ein. Daneben besteht zusätzlich ein kleineres Haus, das Moretti-Theater, die spätere Wirkungsstätte Carl Maria von Webers. Die Einweihung von Gottfried Sempers Neubau als »Erstes Königliches Hoftheater« erfolgte 1841 mit Webers *Jubelouvertüre* und Goethes *Torquato Tasso*. Die überlebensgroßen Sitzfiguren von Dramatikern wie Shakespeare und Moliere (neben Goethe und Schiller) weisen auf die Doppelfunktion als Musik- und Sprechtheater hin. Bereits 1869 vernichtet ein Brand das »schönste Theater der Welt«, in dem der gefeierte Hofkapellmeister Richard Wagner seine Werke *Rienzi*, *Der fliegende Holländer* und *Tannhäuser* zur Uraufführung brachte. Ein Interimstheater überbrückte die Zeit bis zur Eröffnung des zweiten »Königlichen Hoftheaters« 1878, von Gottfried Semper unter Mitwirkung seines Sohnes Manfred errichtet. Das prachtvolle Gebäude, in Anlehnung an die italienische Hochrenaissance gebaut, gleicht einem »Theaterschloss«. Eine zweigeschossige Bogenarchitektur an der Frontseite und das hervorspringende Eingangsportal betonen den festlichen Charakter des Hauses. Hier wurden mit den Uraufführungen der Opern von Richard Strauss, dem Wirken der Dirigenten Ernst von Schuch, Fritz Busch und in jüngster Zeit Giuseppe Sinopoli Tradition und Innovation gleichermaßen gepflegt.

Dresden without the Semper Opera House is unthinkable! The "Electoral Opera House on Taschenberg" from 1667 was the first in a long line of houses and was situated near the royal palace. On the occasion of his son's marriage in 1719, Augustus the Strong had Italian architects, assisted by Pöppelmann, build the "Large Opera House" at the Zwinger which became the center of baroque operatic art in Germany. The composers Johann Adolf Hasse and Johann Gottlieb Naumann ("the divine Saxon") ushered in a glittering era of musical performance. Next to the splendid "Large Opera House", a smaller house, the Moretti Theatre, was also built. Carl Maria von Weber later worked there. Gottfried Semper's new opera house, the "First Royal Court Theatre", opened in 1841 with Weber's *Jubilee Overture* and Goethe's *Torquato Tasso*. The monuments to dramatists such as Shakespeare and Molière, besides Goethe and Schiller, indicate that this is a theatre for the performance of plays *and* operas. The "world's loveliest theatre" was destroyed by fire in 1869, however. Richard Wagner was the court music director at Dresden for a time and he staged the premieres of his own *Rienzi*, *The Flying Dutchman* and *Tannhäuser* here. Another theatre was used temporarily until the second "Royal Court Theatre" opened in 1878. Again it was the work of Gottfried Semper, this time assisted by his son Manfred. The magnificent building is modelled on the Italian High Renaissance and has the appearance of a "theatre palace". Its two-story arcade and the projecting entrance underline the festive purpose of the house. The premieres of operas by Richard Strauss, the work of conductors Ernst von Schuch, Fritz Busch and, more recently, Giuseppe Sinopoli are a few examples of how tradition and innovation are cultivated in equal measure here.

Die Panterquadriga von Johannes Schilling bekrönt die Exedra am Eingangsportal der Semperoper.
Johannes Schilling's quadriga of panthers crowns the exedra of the entrance of the Semper Opera House.

1985 wurde das Opernhaus mit Webers *Freischütz* glanzvoll wiedereröffnet.
In 1985 the Opera House was gloriously re-opened with Weber's *Freischütz*.

Generationen namhafter Baumeister haben an diesem Monument sächsischer Geschichte Spuren hinterlassen. Die Residenz wurde bis zur Revolution 1918 von den Wettinern bewohnt, danach war der Gebäudekomplex mit der Schatzkammer – »Grünes Gewölbe« genannt – bis zur Zerstörung 1945 Museum. Nachdem Anfang der neunziger Jahre Haube und Spitze des Hausmannsturms wieder aufgesetzt wurden und einige Flügel sowie das Georgentor ausgebaut sind, steht der Erweiterung der Staatlichen Kunstsammlungen nichts mehr im Wege. So wird als erstes die umfangreiche Sammlung des Kupferstich-Kabinetts ins Schloss einziehen, gefolgt vom Grünen Gewölbe, das 2004 umziehen wird. Auch die Rüstkammer – eine der schönsten Prunkwaffensammlungen der Welt – und das Münzkabinett erhalten Ausstellungsräume im Schloss. Das Grüne Gewölbe als Herzstück der weitreichenden kunsthandwerklichen Expositionen wurde nach Plänen Augusts des Starken zum ersten musealen Gesamtkunstwerk der Welt erweitert. Bezugnehmend auf das Meisterwerk des Goldschmieds und Juweliers Johann Melchior Dinglinger *Der Hofstaat des Großmoguls Aureng-Zeb* schrieb ein Bewunderer: »Man glaubt sich in den Zauberpalast eines orientalischen Feenmärchens versetzt.« Sonderausstellungen und Theateraufführungen in der ehemaligen Schützkapelle verheißen bereits jetzt eine Neubelebung dieses stilistisch vielgestaltigen historischen Ortes. So ziert die Westfassade im Großen Schlosshof eine rekonstruierte Sgraffito-Bemalung aus der Renaissance, während die Fassadengestaltung des Schlosses aus Anlass des Wettiner Jubiläums Ende des 19. Jahrhunderts einheitlich im Stil der Neorenaissance erneuert wurde.

Renowned master builders have left their mark on Dresden's royal palace over the centuries. Until the 1918 Revolution, it was the residence of the House of Wettin; thereafter, the complex housed the royal treasure vault until it was destroyed in 1945. At the beginning of the 1990s, the Hausmann Tower, the Georgen Gate and some of the palace's wings were restored. When completed, the palace will be home to Saxony's art collection. The first part to move in will be the large collection of copperplate engravings. One of the world's most impressive collections of weapons, the Rüstkammer (Armoury), and the Numismatic Collection are also due to re-open there. 2004 sees the re-opening in its original location of the Grünes Gewölbe (Green Vault), the largest and most magnificent treasury in Europe that Augustus the Strong opened as the world's first treasure museum. Comprising artifacts of gold, silver, precious stones, ivory, emerald and bronze, this stunning collection survived the war intact, having been evacuated to Königstein fortress upriver. The collection's undoubted centerpiece is *The Royal Household at Delhi on the Birthday of the Great Mogul.* A masterly miniature recreation of the court of the Mogul Emperor Aurengzeb, it took the court jeweller Johann Melchior Dinglinger, and others, eight years to complete. Special exhibitions and theatre performances in the chapel where the "father of German music" Heinrich Schütz worked have already breathed new life into a historic venue characterised by a variety of styles. A restored example of Renaissances sgraffito decoration graces its west façade in the large courtyard, for instance. The palace façade was renovated in neo-Renaissance style to mark a Wettin anniversary at the end of the nineteenth century.

Der Stallhofgang des Dresdener Schlosses nach der Zerstörung.
The ruined Stallhof arcade in the Royal Palace.

Rekonstruierte Teile neben Ruinen an der Ostseite des Schlosses.
Reconstructed sections alongside ruins on the east side of the Royal Palace.

Blick in den großen Schlosshof mit dem Hausmannsturm.
View of the large Palace courtyard with the Hausmann Tower.

Kathedrale St. Trinitatis (ehemalige Katholische Hofkirche)

St. Trinitatis Cathedral (former Catholic Hofkirche)

Auf dem Dach der katholischen Kirche scheinen »in immer gesteigerterer Extase Heilige und Engel mit wehenden Gewändern den Himmel zu stürmen.« Lebhaft erinnert sich eine Dresdenerin auch an die »herrlichen Kirchengesänge, an denen der Chor und die Großen Solisten der Oper mitwirkten«. Die *Krönungsmesse* von Mozart oder Orgelkonzerte auf der historischen Orgel von Gottfried Silbermann stimmen auch heute noch viele Besucher festlich. Bau und Weihe der Hofkirche widerspiegeln eines der spannendsten Kapitel sächsischer Geschichte. Mit der Krönung Augusts des Starken zum polnischen König 1697 konvertierte der protestantische Landesherr zum Katholizismus. Seinem Nachfolger war es ein Bedürfnis, als würdiges Pendant zum mächtigen Kuppelbau der evangelischen Frauenkirche eine Hofkirche am Altstädter Brückenkopf zu errichten. Den Auftrag dazu bekam der römische Architekt Gaetano Chiaveri, der 1738 mit dem Bauwerk begann, das erst 1754 fertig gestellt wurde. Die dreischiffige Basilika im Stil des römischen Spätbarock wird durch einen 86 Meter hohen, schlank wirkenden Turm gekrönt, der als Wahrzeichen die Stadtsilhouette bereichert. Als Prozessionsgang für die Gläubigen dienen die beiden ausladenden Seitenschiffe, die das Mittelschiff umschließen. Auf den Balustraden der Kirche stehen wieder die überlebensgroßen, im Krieg stark beschädigten Sandsteinfiguren von Lorenzo Matielli. Im Inneren verdient die vom Bildhauer Balthasar Permoser geschaffene Kanzel Bewunderung. Die ehemalige Hofkirche wurde 1980 zur Kathedrale des Bistums Dresden-Meißen erhoben.

"Atop the Catholic cathedral, the saints and angels, their robes flowing, appear to storm heavenwards in heightened ecstasy" in the recollection of one Dresden woman who also vividly recalls the "magnificent hymns sung by the cathedral choir and famous soloists from the Opera". Mozart's *Coronation Mass* or organ recitals given on the historic instrument by Gottfried Silbermann deeply impress visitors to this day. The construction and dedication of the Hofkirche reflect one of the most exciting chapters in the history of Saxony: when Protestant Augustus the Strong was crowned king of Poland in 1697, he converted to Roman Catholicism. For the use of the royal court, his successor felt the need to build a worthy counterpart to the massive dome of the Protestant Frauenkirche in Neumarkt, and the commission was awarded to the Roman architect Gaetano Chiaveri. Work on the church overlooking the Augustus Bridge started in 1738 and was completed in 1754. In late Roman baroque style, the three-bay basilica sits beneath an 86-metre-high spire that appears graceful despite its height. It embellishes the skyline and has long been a symbol of the city. The larger-than-life-size sandstone figures positioned around the balustrades are again the work of Lorenzo Mattielli. Inside the church, Balthasar Permoser's wonderful baroque pulpit draws admiring glances. In 1980, the former court church became the Cathedral Church of the diocese of Dresden and Meissen.

Heiligenfiguren auf dem Dach der stark beschädigten Katholischen Hofkirche mit Blick zum Theaterplatz.
Figures of saints atop the roof of the badly damaged Catholic Hofkirche, view towards Theaterplatz.

»Canalettoblick« vom Turm der Dreikönigskirche.
Made famous by Canaletto: the view from the spire of the Church of the Epiphany.

Die Kathedrale St. Trinitatis am Altstädter Brückenkopf der Augustusbrücke.
St. Trinitatis Catholic Cathedral opposite the Augustus Bridge.

Taschenbergpalais

Taschenbergpalais

Auf ältestem Siedlungsboden steht Dresdens schönstes Stadtpalais – das Taschenbergpalais. Es ist noch nicht einmal ein Jahrzehnt her, da standen von dem Prachtbau aus augusteischer Zeit nur noch geschwärzte Umfassungsmauern und Birken wuchsen aus den Ruinen. Heute zählt es zu den exklusivsten Hotels der Stadt. Barock und Rokoko prägten das 1705 nach Entwürfen von Pöppelmann und anderen Baumeistern direkt neben dem Schloss errichtete Palais. Der Grund war pikanter Natur: Der liebestrunkene König brauchte ein luxuriöses Liebesnest für seine Mätresse Anna Constantia von Cosel, wegen ihrer Schönheit und Klugheit geschätzt und gefürchtet zugleich. Doch schon 1713 fiel sie in Ungnade und musste die Residenz verlassen. Die Geschichten um die Gräfin Cosel, die kein Stadtführer auslässt, sind immer noch in aller Munde und wurden von Literatur und Film aufgegriffen. Nach dem Ende der Affäre diente das Palais als Residenz für den Kurprinzen, der als guter Katholik eine Hauskapelle einbauen ließ und den Kernbau durch Flügelbauten und Ehrenhöfe beträchtlich erweiterte. Bis auf die barocke Treppenanlage, die wiederhergestellt wurde, ist davon nichts mehr vorhanden. Im 19. Jahrhundert wurde mit der Schlosserneuerung auch das baufällig gewordene Taschenbergpalais verändert und das hohe Mansarddach (1995 wiederhergestellt) durch ein Flachdach ersetzt. Der Flügel am östlichen Ehrenhof, in dem ein gemütlicher Bierausschank geöffnet hat, ist durch einen brückenähnlichen Übergang mit dem Schloss verbunden. Am Eingang zum Sophienkeller steht ein neugotischer Brunnen, der 1843 nach Plänen Gottfried Sempers errichtet wurde, zum Dank, dass die Cholera die Stadt verschont hatte.

Standing in the oldest part of the city, the Taschenberg Palace is once more Dresden's loveliest palace. Not even a decade has passed since only its blackened outer walls stood here, but it has now been transformed into one of the city's most exclusive hotels. To plans by Pöppelmann and others, it was built in 1705 in baroque and rococo styles immediately beside the Royal Palace – with good reason. The King needed a love nest for his mistress, Anna Constantia von Cosel, a woman both admired and feared for her beauty and intelligence. Yet she fell out of favour with the King in 1713 and had to leave the palace. She is still talked about to this day and no tour guide would want to omit the tales surrounding her. They have even been the subject of books and movies. After her departure, the Taschenberg Palace became the official home of the heir to the throne. A good Catholic, he installed a private chapel and had wings and *cours d'honneur* added to the core building. None of this survives except for the rebuilt baroque staircase. When the Royal Palace was renovated in the nineteenth century, alterations were also made to the dilapidated Taschenberg Palace. Among other things, its tall double mansards were replaced with hip roofs. The mansards were restored in 1995. The Royal Palace is connected by footbridge to the east wing of the Taschenberg Palace in whose *cour d'honneur* there is now a pleasant bar. At the entrance to the Sophienkeller restaurant there is a neo-gothic fountain designed by Semper in 1843. Called the Cholera Fountain, it was erected to give thanks for the city being spared a cholera epidemic.

Das Taschenbergpalais zwischen Residenzschloss und Zwinger.
The Taschenberg Palace between the Royal Palace and the Zwinger.

Die reiche Fassadengestaltung ist typisch für dieses Meisterwerk des Dresdener Barock.
Rich ornamentation is typical for this masterpiece of Dresden Baroque.

Brühlsche Terrasse

Brühlsche Terrasse

Als »Kunsttempel für die Brühlsche Terrasse« wurde die Monumentalarchitektur des Kunstausstellungs- und Kunstakademiegebäudes von Konstantin Lipsius anlässlich ihrer Einweihung 1894 gefeiert. Die räumlich großzügig gestalteten Zweckbauten erfüllen für Studierende und Lehrende diesen Anspruch bis heute. An dieser exponierten Stelle auf dem Gelände des Brühlschen Gartens, auf den wuchtigen Festungsmauern des alten Dresdens, haben in Ost-West-Ausrichtung zur Elbe hin vier namhafte Architekten gebaut, aber nur Gustav Frölich bewahrte den Genius Loci, in dem er das Gebäude der »Sekundogenitur« in barocker Formensprache nachempfand. Der Umbau zum neuen Ausstellungsgebäude begann 1896 und wurde noch vor Baubeginn des neuen Ständehauses (heute Gericht) abgeschlossen. Architekt des Ständehauses war der Schöpfer des Berliner Reichstagsgebäudes Paul Wallot. Wallots Verdienst besteht darin, dass er den Turm des Ständehauses asymmetrisch zur Elbfront anlegte und somit die Achse vom Georgentor am Altstädter Brückenkopf über die Augustusbrücke in die Neustadt in ihrer Wirkung beließ. Damit wurde gleichzeitig ein städtebaulich ausgewogenes Gegengewicht zur Hofkirche in Richtung Schlossplatz geschaffen. Beibehalten wurde die raumgreifende Freitreppe von Gottlob Friedrich Thormeyer mit den vier Plastiken der *Tageszeiten* von Johannes Schilling. Das östliche Ende der Terrasse wird durch das Albertinum (so genannt nach dem Umbau des ehemaligen Zeughauses durch Karl Adolf Canzler) und das ehemalige Hofgärtnerhaus, das heute eine reformierte Kirche beherbergt, abgeschlossen.

At their official opening in 1894, the monumental Art Gallery and Art Academy by Konstantin Lipsius were celebrated as temples of art on the Brühlsche Terrasse. These generously proportioned, purpose-built buildings meet the needs of students and professors alike. Four architects were commsioned to build atop the old city fortifications, an exposed position with an east-west orientation overlooking the river, but only Gustav Frölich suceeded in retaining the character of the place by modelling his Sekundogenitur on Baroque forms. The old Academy was to be re-developed as a new exhibition space. Work began in 1896 and was completed before the start of building work on the new parliament house (Neues Ständehaus, now a court), built by Paul Wallot, the architect of the Reichstag in Berlin. It is to Wallot's credit that he placed the tower of the Ständehaus at an angle to the river, thus preserving the sight lines at the Altstädter bridge head from the Georgentor, the Augustus Bridge across to Neustadt. By doing so, in town planning terms he also created a harmonious counterpoise to the Hofkirche that overlooks the Schlossplatz. Gottlob Friedrich Thormeyer's extensive flight of stairs with its sculptures of the *Times of the Day* by Johannes Schilling was retained. The Albertinum, home to some of the city's most famous art treasures, and the former Hofgärtnerhaus (now a reformed church) complete the eastern end of the Terrace.

Blick über die Brühlsche Terrasse elbaufwärts mit Carola- und Albertbrücke, Vorkriegsaufnahme.
Looking upstream across the Brühlsche Terrasse towards the Carola- and Albert Bridges, pre-war photograph.

Phantasus von Robert Henze auf dem Seitenrisalit der Kunstakademie.
Robert Henze's *Phantasus* atop the Academy of Fine Art.

Blick über die Brühlsche Terrasse elbabwärts, im Vordergrund die
Kuppel der Kunstakademie.
Looking upriver across the Brühlsche Terrasse, in the foreground,
the dome of the Academy of Fine Art.

Neue Synagoge

New Synagogue

Eng mit dem Geistes- und Geschäftsleben Dresdens war das Wirken bedeutender jüdischer Persönlichkeiten verbunden. Hervorzuheben sind die Bankhäuser Oppenheim und Gebrüder Arnhold, die sich vor allem als Kunstmäzene verdient gemacht haben. Berühmt sind auch die Tagebücher des Literaturwissenschaftlers Victor Klemperer, in denen auf erschütternde Weise der Alltag während der Nazidiktatur lebendig wird. Vor 1933 zählte die jüdische Gemeinde rund 6000 Mitglieder, 1945 waren es noch zwölf, die den Holocaust überlebt hatten. Der Alte Jüdische Friedhof (Pulsnitzer Straße), der unter Denkmalschutz steht, und der Neue Jüdische Friedhof an der Fiedlerstraße, auf dem sich seit 1950 eine kleine Synagoge befand, bewahren die Erinnerung an die jüdischen Mitbürger. 1838/40 hatte Gottfried Semper im Auftrag der Jüdischen Gemeinde in Elbnähe eine Synagoge gebaut, die in der Pogromnacht 1938 zerstört wurde, nur der Davidstern konnte gerettet werden. Die Neue Synagoge zwischen Brühlscher Terrasse und Carolabrücke bricht mit der Dresdener Architekturtradition. Das in Saarbrücken und Frankfurt a.M. ansässige Büro Wandel Hoefer Lorch + Hirsch schuf den Sakralbau als einen homogenen, massigen Kubus, der in seiner Geschlossenheit an alttestamentarische Bauformen erinnert, während die verglaste Nordfassade des Gemeindehauses zum Innenhof Transparenz zeigt. Das zur Verfügung stehende Grundstück verhinderte die Ausrichtung der Synagoge nach Osten. Architektonisch verblüffend einfach wurde das Problem gelöst, indem man das Gebäude in sich verdrehte. Im Kontrast zum schmucklosen, massiven Äußeren erscheint der edel gestaltete Innenraum, der die Gemeinde unter einem fragilen Metallzelt vereint. Die Vergabe des Architekturpreises der Deutschen Kritiker 2001 würdigte den Entwurf.

The worlds of business and learning in Dresden were closely associated with the work of important Jewish institutions and personalities. Prominent among them were the Oppenheim and Arnhold banking houses that gained a reputation as patrons of the arts. The diaries of the literary scholar Victor Klemperer, who taught in Dresden for 15 years before being suspended in 1935, present a distressing portrait of daily life as a Jew under the Nazi dictatorship. Before 1933, Dresden's Jewish congregation numbered about 6,000; in 1945, there were only twelve survivors. The Old Jewish Cemetery in Pulsnitzerstrasse (now under a preservation order), and the New Jewish Cemetery in Fiedlerstrasse (where there has been a small synagogue since 1950), are powerful reminders of the men and women of the Jewish faith who once lived here. From 1838–40, Gottfried Semper built a synagogue near the Elbe. Except for its Star of David, it was destroyed in the pogrom of November 1938. The New Synagogue is located between Brühlscher Terrasse and Carola Bridge, and breaks with the city's architectural traditions. Wandel Hoefer Lorch + Hirsch, Architects (Saarbrücken and Frankfurt am Main) have created a religious building in the shape of a massive, uniform cube whose self-contained quality is reminiscent of the buildings described in the Old Testament. The community centre's glazed north wall overlooking the inner courtyard suggests transparency. The orientation of the building plot was such that the ark would not face east, a problem cleverly solved simply by "twisting" the building. Its plain and massive exterior forms a striking contrast with the rich interior that unites the congregation beneath a fine metal canopy. The architects were awarded the German Architectural Critics' Prize for their design.

Die Synagoge von Gottfried Semper, Stahlstich von 1850.
Gottfried Semper's Synagogue, steel engraving from 1850.

Westfassade der Neuen Synagoge. Im linken Gebäudeteil befindet sich der Synagogenraum, rechts das Gemeindehaus.
The west façade of the New Synagogue. The synagogue is on the left, the community centre on the right.

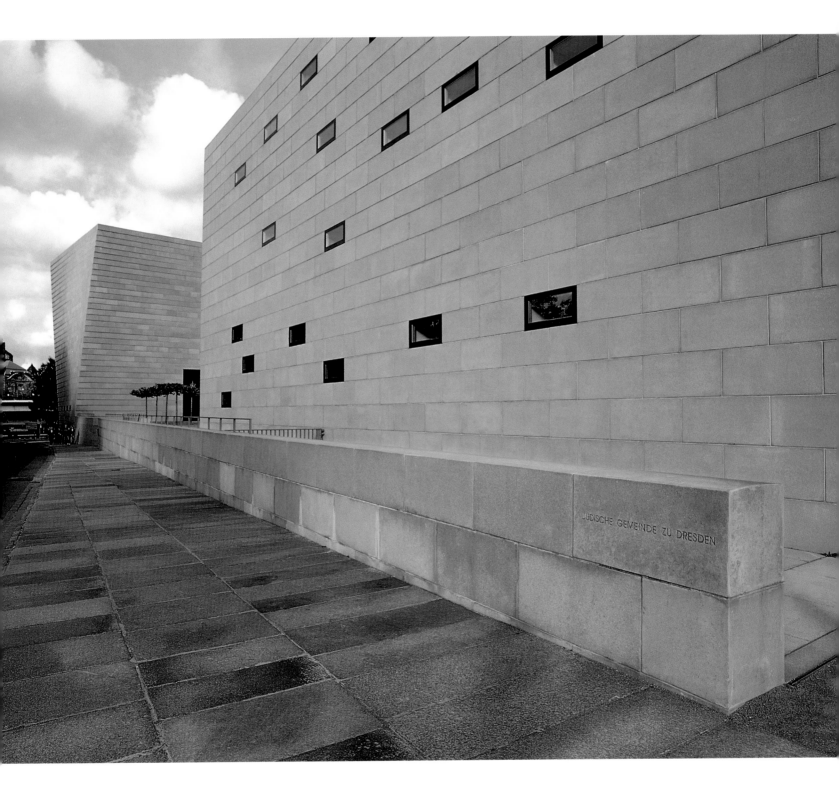

Frauenkirche und Neumarkt

Frauenkirche and Neumarkt

Die barocke Frauenkirche, zwischen 1726 und 1743 vom Ratszimmermeister George Bähr erbaut und im Bombenhagel des 13. Februar 1945 so schwer beschädigt, dass sie später einstürzte, verdankt ihre Wiedererrichtung einem bisher nicht gekannten Gemeinsinn, der sich durch weltweite Spenden ausdrückt. Das vergoldete Kuppelkreuz neben dem Lutherdenkmal beispielsweise wurde vom Dresden Trust aus Großbritannien gestiftet. Nach der archäologischen Bergung verwendbarer Steine aus dem Trümmerberg erfolgte ab 1994 die stufenweise Rekonstruktion des sakralen Bauwerks mittels alter Handwerkskunst und modernster Technologien. Unter den strengen Augen der Denkmalpflege wird die Wunde im Herzen Dresdens geheilt und dennoch die Erinnerung an die Zerstörung vom Februar 1945 nicht ausgelöscht. Neu an dem historischen Bau, der wegen des geschwungenen Kuppelansatzes auch »Steinerne Glocke« genannt wird, ist die Nutzung der kreuzförmigen Tonnengewölbe als Unterkirche und der sich hufeneisenförmig anschmiegende unterirdische Außenanbau für Garderoben und Haustechnik. Nachdem die Gerüste an den Fassaden bis zur Kuppel hinauf gefallen sind, wird klar, dass der nach 1945 großflächig abgeräumte Neumarkt um die Frauenkirche eine kleinteilige, aber städtebaulich vertretbare Ergänzung haben muss. Mit dem Coselpalais und seinem repräsentativen Ehrenhof wurde bereits ein so genannter Leitbau zurückgewonnen, dem weitere Bürgerhäuser im Zusammenspiel mit zeitgenössischer Architektur folgen sollen. In unmittelbarer Nachbarschaft befindet sich das bislang noch ruinöse Kurländer Palais, das künftig multifunktional genutzt werden soll. Das Verkehrsmuseum, nach seinem Umbau von der Gemäldegalerie zur Rüstkammer im 19. Jahrhundert Johanneum genannt, begrenzt den Neumarkt an der Westseite.

The baroque Frauenkirche, erected by George Bähr between 1726–43, is now benefiting from a new public spirit that has found expression in worldwide donations towards its reconstruction. It was destroyed by Allied bombs in February 1945. The new Orb and Cross beside Luther's memorial, for instance, is the gift of the people of Britain, and was presented to the Dresden Foundation by HRH the Duke of Kent on behalf of the Dresden Trust. During archaeological clearance work at the site, reusable stone was salvaged from the pile of rubble. Reconstruction work began in 1994 and made use of the ancient skills of craftsmen and the latest technology. A start has finally been made on repairing the wounds in the heart of Dresden, even if memories of the church's destruction in February 1945 cannot be erased. The sweeping dome is now beginning to rise and has already earned the historic building the nickname of "Stone Bell". For the first time, use is being made of the reconstructed sandstone vaulted crypt that contains a marble altarpiece by British sculptor Amish Kapoor. Technical and supply facilities have been fitted in a construction built underground around the ground plan of the building. With scaffolding gradually coming down, it is now apparent that as much as possible of the historic Neumarkt surrounding the Frauenkirche needs to be restored. A start has been made by rebuilding the Cosel Palace with its representative *cour d'honneur*; other baroque houses are to follow. The ruined Kurländer Palace is situated nearby; when restored, it will contain representative rooms, restaurants and apartments. The Verkehrsmuseum (Transport Museum), following its conversion from gallery to armoury in the nineteenth century, and named the Johanneum in honour of King Johann, completes the western end of the Neumarkt.

Die Ruine der Frauenkirche – Mahnmal gegen den Krieg, Aufnahme von 1963.
The ruined Frauenkirche in 1963 – a monument to the horrors of war.

Die Baustelle der Frauenkirche auf dem Neumarkt.
In Neumarkt, the construction site of the Frauenkirche.

Oben: Für den Wiederaufbau werden auch aus den Trümmern geborgene Steine verwendet.
Unten: Links ein Renaissanceportal, die »Schöne Pforte«, aus der Schlosskapelle.
Top: Stone salvaged from its ruins has been used in its reconstruction.
Bottom: On the left is the Renaissance gateway called the "Schöne Pforte" from the Palace chapel.

Coselpalais und Verkehrsmuseum (Johanneum)

Cosel Palace and Transport Museum (Johanneum)

Das Coselpalais, unmittelbar neben der Frauenkirche, steht als Beispiel für einen äußerlich detailgetreu wiederhergestellten Adelspalast des Augusteischen Zeitalters. 1745/46 errichtete Oberlandbaumeister Johann Christoph Knöffel an dieser Stelle zwei mehrgeschossige Gebäude, die 1760 bei der Beschießung Dresdens durch die Preußen stark beschädigt wurden. Nach dem Wechsel der Besitzer diente es als Wohnsitz für General Graf Friedrich August Cosel, einen Sohn Augusts des Starken und der Gräfin Cosel. Der prächtigen Hauptfassade (Architekt Julius Heinrich Schwarze) mit dem Dreiecksgiebel über dem Mittelrisalit und den Rundbögen mit Trophäenbekrönung lagert ein repräsentativer Ehrenhof mit zwei Seitenflügeln vor. Nach dem Wiederaufbau wird das Palais als Restaurant genutzt, Reste der mittelalterlichen Stadtbefestigung wurden in den Neubau integriert.

Auf den Renaissancecharakter des ursprünglich von Paul Buchner und Hans Ermisch für den kurfürstlichen Hof errichteten Stallgebäudes (1586–1591) weisen nur noch die beiden wuchtigen Portale an der Vorderfront sowie an der Nordwestseite und die Kappengewölbe im Erdgeschoss hin. Unter August dem Starken und seinem Sohn wurde der Bau zwischen 1729 und 1731 für die Aufnahme der königlichen Kunstsammlung umgebaut. Bereits 1744 gestaltete Knöffel die Galerie noch einmal um und schuf u.a. die doppelläufige Englische Treppe, die auf Canalettos Gemälde zu sehen ist. Aus dem 17. Jahrhundert stammt der achteckige Friedens- oder Türkenbrunnen. Die Friedensgöttin wurde 1689 durch eine Victoria ersetzt, die an den Sieg des Kurfürsten Johann Georg III. über die Türken erinnert. Den Namen »Johanneum« verdankt das nach 1952 eingerichtete Verkehrsmuseum dem Bauherrn König Johann, der nach dem Auszug der Gemäldegalerie 1872 bis 1877 dort wieder die Rüstkammer und die Porzellangalerie unterbringen ließ.

Dating from the era of Augustus the Strong, the Cosel Palace sits alongside the Frauenkirche and is an example of an aristocratic residence with a painstakingly restored exterior. Here in 1745–46, the state architect Johann Christoph Knöffel built a pair of two-storey buildings that were badly damaged by Prussian artillery fire in 1760. They later became the home of General Graf Friedrich August Cosel, a son of Augustus the Strong and Countess Cosel. Julius Heinrich Schwarze was the architect of the building whose splendid main façade has a gabled central section and arched and oval windows. The two-storey wings enclose a representative courtyard; arches surmounted by trophies sit over their central window axes. Following its recent reconstruction, the Palace is used as a restaurant.

Only two remaining gateways, one to the front and one in the northwest wall, and the vaults in the basement, recall the Renaissance origins of this building that housed the Elector's stables, built by Paul Buchner and Hans Ermisch from 1586–91. Under Augustus the Strong and his son, the building was remodelled between 1729 and 1731 as a home for the royal art collection; shortly after, in 1744, the gallery was again re-designed, but by Knöffel. The double flight of the Englische Treppe (English Steps), seen in Canaletto's painting, dates from this time. The octagonal Peace or Turkish Fountain dates from the seventeenth century. A statue of the goddess of peace was replaced in 1689 by a figure of Victory to commemorate Elector Johann Georg III's participation in the successful defence of Vienna against the Turks. The name "Johanneum" honours King John, the man who commissioned the building. The Transport Museum first made use of it in 1952. Between 1872–77, the Gemäldegalerie (art collection) moved out, allowing the Rüstkammer (armoury) and the Porcelaine Collection to be housed there.

Verkehrsmuseum (Johanneum) mit doppelläufiger Englischer Treppe.
The Transport Museum (Johanneum) and the double flight of the English Steps.

Bernardo Bellotto, *Der Neumarkt in Dresden vom Jüdenhof aus*, 1749/51.
Bernardo Bellotto, *Dresden's Neumarkt from the Jüdenhof*, 1749/51.

Die Putten auf den Torsäulen stammen vom Hofbildhauer Gottfried Knöffler.
The putti atop the entrance columns are by the court sculptor Gottfried Knöffler.

Zwischen Hauptbahnhof und Altmarkt

Flächendeckend war dieses Areal mit der europaweit berühmten Prager Straße bei den Luftangriffen am 13. Februar 1945 zerstört und in den Nachkriegsjahren enttrümmert worden. Erst in den sechziger Jahren begann man, die Prager Straße als Verbindung zwischen Hauptbahnhof und dem überdimensionierten Altmarkt nach einem städtebaulichen Wettbewerb in Stahlbetonkonstruktion und Großplattenbauweise wiederzuerrichten. Die Eintönigkeit, durch den geradlinigen Verlauf ohne Unterbrechung von Querstraßen provoziert, wird lediglich durch den zylindrischen Bau des Rundkinos und das dekonstruktivistische Ufa-Kinozentrum von Coop Himmelb(l)au aufgelockert. Unverwechselbare Anhaltspunkte bleiben der Hauptbahnhof am südlichen Ende und das zwischen 1905 und 1910 errichtete Neue Rathaus, die Kreuzkirche sowie die ehemalige Bankfiliale an der Ringstraße, ein Stahlskelettbau mit vorgeblendeten Sandsteinfassaden, in nördlicher Richtung. Die Kaufhäuser und Bürogebäude der neunziger Jahre sind variationsreiche Versuche, das dicht bebaute Stadtzentrum der Vorkriegszeit wiederherzustellen. Im Zuge des Wiederaufbaus nach dem Krieg mit einem großräumigen sozialistischen Stadtzentrum mit Aufmarschplätzen und überbreiten Straßen wurde die Grundfläche des Altmarktes um das Dreifache erweitert. An der Westseite wurde mit den Arkaden an die barocke Dresdener Bautradition angeknüpft. Auch die Verwendung des regional typischen Sandsteins greift traditionelle Bauweisen auf. Die übergroße Platzfläche, auf der alljährlich zur Weihnachtszeit der Dresdener Striezelmarkt stattfindet, wird durch Wohn- und Geschäftsbauten allmählich verkleinert. An der Nordseite wartet der als Konzerthalle für Philharmonie und Staatskapelle genutzte Kulturpalast von 1969 auf den geplanten Umbau.

From the Main Railway Station to Altmarkt

The whole of this area, including a street famed throughout Europe, Prager Strasse (Prague Street), was destroyed in air-raids on 13–14 February 1945. The resulting heaps of rubble were cleared away in the post-war years. Following an architectural competition, it was the 1960s before work, using reinforced concrete and large panel construction methods, began on the reconstruction of Prager Strasse as the thoroughfare connecting the main railway station (Hauptbahnhof) and the immense space of Altmarkt. Its straight lines and the lack of side streets produce a sense of monotony that is relieved only by the new deconstructionist multiplex cinema of the Viennese firm Coop Himmelb(l)au. The only remaining unmistakable reference points are the main railway station, built from 1905–10, the Neues Rathaus (new town hall), the Kreuzkirche and the former bank on Ringstrasse, a steel-framed structure with a sandstone frontage. With the department stores and office blocks built in the 1990s, various attempts have been made to re-create the former density of building found in the city centre. The result of the development of a vast, socialist centre with parade grounds and excessively wide streets is seen in the pseudo-baroque buildings erected around the square, whose size the East German authorities increased by a third. The arcades along its western side are impressive, however, because they carry on a Dresden tradition. New buildings have more or less reduced the area of the Altmarkt, which is incidentally the venue for Dresden's Christmas market. On the north side of Altmarkt, the 1969 Kulturpalast (Palace of Culture) is a now inadequate concert hall used by the Dresden Philharmonic and the Staatskapelle. It is to be hoped that its long-planned refurbishment will improve its external appearance, too.

Der Altmarkt mit Kreuzkirche und Rathausturm im Hintergrund, Vorkriegsaufnahme.
Altmarkt with the Kreuzkirche and the town hall tower in the background, pre-war photograph.

Denkmal für die Dresdener Trümmerfrauen vor dem Neuen Rathaus von Walter Reinhold, 1952.
This memorial by Walter Reinhold, 1952, to the women who cleared away the rubble of the ruined city ("Trümmerfrauen") stands in front of the New Town Hall.

Oben: Ostseite des Altmarkts mit Blick nach Norden zur Frauenkirche.
Unten: Die Wilsdruffer Straße mit dem Kulturpalast.
Top: The east side of Altmarkt looking north towards the Frauenkirche.
Bottom: Wilsdruffer Strasse with the Palace of Culture.

Springbrunnen auf der Prager Straße.
Fountain in Prager Strasse.

»Haus des Buches« am Dr.-Külz-Ring.
"The Home of the Book" on Dr.-Külz-Ring.

UFA-Kinozentrum von Coop Himmelb(l)au, in der Spiegelung
ist das Rundkino von 1972 zu sehen.
UFA cinema by Coop Himmelb(l)au; the 1972 circular cinema
is seen in the reflection.

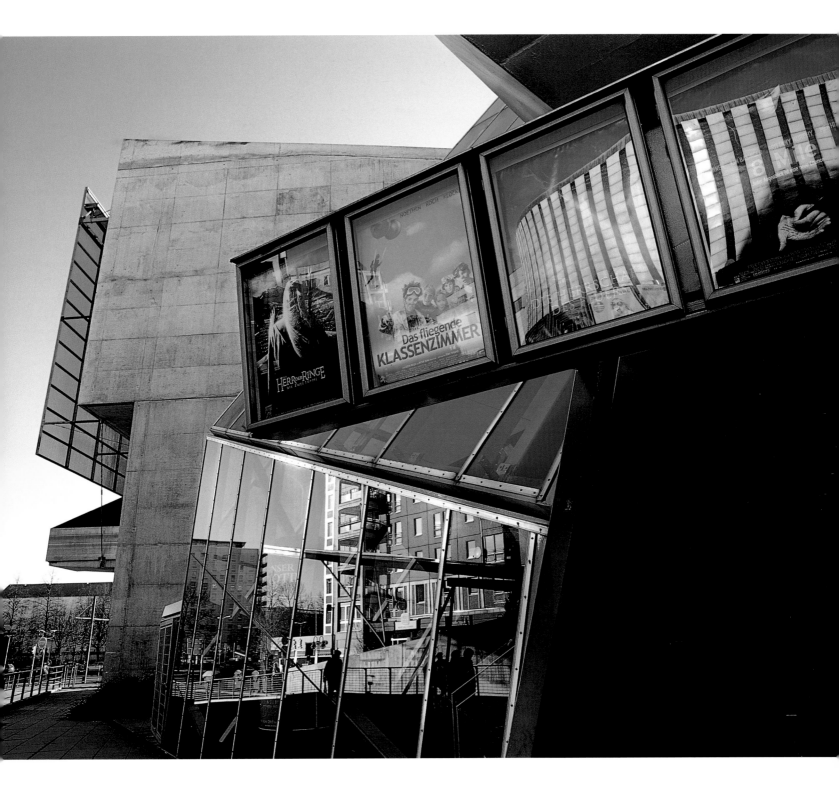

Neuer Landtag und Kongresszentrum

Als Leitbild für eine moderne Architektur, die Respekt vor dem historischen Umfeld zeigt, passt sich Peter Kulkas neuer Landtag von 1994 in die abwechslungsreich gegliederte Achse, die sich von der Brühlschen Terrasse westlich in Richtung Marienbrücke als historische »Kulturmeile« erstreckt, bruchlos ein. Gelungen auch, wie der Architekt das von 1928 bis 1931 errichtete Landesfinanzamt – früher Sitz der SED-Bezirksleitung – funktionell in seine großzügige Stahlkonstruktion einbezieht. Die Form des transparenten Gebäudes erinnert an Mies van der Rohes Neue Nationalgalerie in Berlin. Hervorgerufen wird dieser Eindruck vor allem durch den Plenarsaal, der in eigenständiger Ecklage, nur geringfügig höher gestaffelt als der öffentlich zugängliche Elbflügel, von einer gekrümmten Glasfassade ummantelt ist. Als Anschlussbau erhebt sich dahinter in kolossaler Stahlbetonbauweise der ehemalige städtische Speicher, nach seinem Erbauer Hans Erlwein »Erlwein-Speicher« genannt. Die Gliederung des Baus durch Aufzugsschächte, die wie Querhäuser hervortreten, prädestinierten den grauen Riesenbau bis vor kurzem noch als idealen Standort für die Sächsische Landesbibliothek. Zur Zeit ist ein Umbau als Hotel für das dahinterliegende neue Kongresszentrum vorgesehen. Dresden hat sich nach 1989 als ein begehrter Standort für internationale Kongresse ausgewiesen, doch bisher fehlte ein modernes Tagungszentrum. Die Architektengruppe Storch & Ehlers, die schon am west-östlichen Architektenworkshop 1990 teilgenommen hatte, erhielt den Zuschlag. Das rohbaufertige Kongresszentrum schließt eine Baulücke in der Altstädter Elbsilhouette. Die gefällige, rampenartig ansteigende Konstruktion zeichnet sich bereits ab und setzt die von Kulka begonnene gemäßigte Dresdener Postmoderne fort.

Peter Kulka's new Saxon Parliament is a model for contemporary architecture that wants to respect its historic surroundings. Built from 1991–94, it fits seamlessly into the "home of culture" between the Brühlsche Terrasse and the Marienbrücke. The architect has also very successfully incorporated into his large steel structure the state finance office, built from 1928–31 and which in G.D.R. days was the headquarters of the regional Communist party. Kulka's building is reminiscent of Mies van der Rohe's New National Gallery in Berlin, an impression given mainly by its plenary chamber surrounded by a curved glass façade and its distinctive corner location. The plenary chamber is slightly raised above the level of the public entrance. Adjacent to it is a monumental reinforced concrete warehouse named after its architect, Hans Erlwein. Elevator shafts are a prominent feature of the building that was considered as a location for the Library of Saxony, but the plan now is to convert it into a hotel for the use of delegates at the new International Congress Centre Dresden a short distance away. Following German unification in 1989, the city began to attract international conferences despite its lack of state-of-the-art facilities. The group of architects Storch & Ehlers who had already participated in the 1990 workshop for architects from east and west was commissioned to design a new congress centre that now fills a gap in the cityscape of the Altstadt district. The attractive, tiered construction is due to open in 2004 and continues the spirit of restrained postmodernism initiated by Kulka.

Der Erlwein-Speicher.
The Warehouse by Hans Erlwein.

Der Neue Landtag mit Kongresszentrum.
Saxony's New Parliament; next door, the Congress Centre is now taking shape.

Blick aus dem Restaurant des Neuen Landtags auf die Altstadtsilhouette.
View of the Old Town from the restaurant in the New Saxon Parliament.

Die Südvorstadt, südlich des Hauptbahnhofs gelegen und sanft ins Erzgebirgsvorland ansteigend, wurde vom Feuersturm des 13. Februar 1945 mit am stärksten betroffen. In der zweiten Hälfte des 19. Jahrhunderts entstanden Villenviertel wie das Schweizer Viertel, von dem einige denkmalgeschützte Bauten erhalten blieben. Das einst von zahlreichen Fremden bewohnte Quartier mit seinen eleganten Mietshäusern für gehobene Ansprüche und rechtwinkelig verlaufenden Straßen hieß im Volksmund das »Amerikanische Viertel«. Als einzige der so genannten Ausländerkirchen blieb die Russisch-Orthodoxe Kirche von 1872/74 mit ihren typischen Zwiebelkuppeln erhalten, die dem Moskauer Patriarchat untersteht. Mit der Südvorstadt eng verbunden ist das Hochschulviertel der Technischen Universität. Die Gebäude des ehemaligen Polytechnikums entstanden bereits um 1875 und wurden nach 1900 durch markante Ziegelbauten erweitert, wobei der turmartige Beyer-Bau mit dem Lohrmann-Observatorium charakteristisch für die alte Technische Hochschule (TH) war, an der bekannte Wissenschaftler und Ingenieure wie Fritz Förster, Heinrich Barkhausen, Wilhelm Hallwachs, Hermann Krone und viele andere als Hochschullehrer wirkten. Nach den verheerenden Kriegsschäden wurde mit dem Wiederaufbau der einzelnen Institute begonnen. Im Zuge der Erweiterung der TU bezog man nach umfangreichen Veränderungen im Gebäudeinneren auch das ehemalige Landgericht, einen burgähnlichen Bau im neuromanischen Stil mit Jugendstilelementen, in das Universitätsgelände ein.

The district of Südvorstadt is situated to the south of Dresden's main railway station and rises gently towards the foothills of the Erzgebirge (Ore Mountains). It was one of the most severely damaged parts of the city following the bombing and firestorm of 13–14 February 1945. In the second half of the nineteenth century, this was an area of villas such as the Swiss Quarter; some of them have survived and are now under preservation orders. A large number of foreigners lived here, a part of town with graceful apartment houses that could satisfy those who required high standards. Laid out on a grid system, it was soon commonly known as the American Quarter. Of the foreign churches once found in Dresden, now only the Russian Orthodox Church survives. Built from 1872–74, it has typical onion domes and is under the Moscow Patriarchate. Dresden's Technical University (TU) is closely associated with Südvorstadt. The buildings that housed the original Polytechnic date from around 1875; after 1900, striking brick buildings were added. The Beyer-Bau, with its observatory tower, is typical of the style of the old polytechnic where notable German scientists and engineers taught. The university's various institutes were rebuilt after the War, in which they were severely damaged. A fortress-like structure in neo-Romanesque style with Jugendstil elements, the former courthouse was converted internally as part of the TU's expansion and is now a campus landmark.

Die Zwiebeltürme der Russisch-Orthodoxen St. Simeons Kirche.
The onion domes of St. Simeon's Russian Orthodox Church.

Auditorium maximum der TU, rechts der Beyer-Bau mit Observatorium.
The auditorium Maximum of the Technical University. On the right is the Beyer-Bau with the Observatory.

Sächsische Landesbibliothek – Staats- und Universitätsbibliothek

Saxony's State Library – State and University Library

Die unaufhaltsame Zunahme diverser Medien wie Bücher, Bild- und Tonträger erfordert zeitgemäße Gebäude für ihre Aufbewahrung und eine moderne Logistik für den raschen Zugriff. Die nach dem Krieg außerhalb des Stadtzentrums in der Albertstadt untergebrachte Landesbibliothek entsprach diesen Anforderungen nicht mehr. Die Bibliothek, die über einen reichen bibliophilen Bestand aus kurfürstlichen Zeiten verfügt, ist seit 2002 mit der Bibliothek der Technischen Universität unter einem Dach vereint. Für den neuen Standort, den Campus am Zelleschen Weg, wurde ein Areal gewählt, auf dem nach 1945 zahlreiche Institute der damaligen Technischen Hochschule entstanden. Die Architekten Ortner & Ortner Baukunst entschieden sich aus funktionellen Gründen für eine teils ober-, teils unterirdische Anordnung der Gebäude. Im unteren Teil sind aufgrund der Lichtempfindlichkeit und aus Sicherheitserwägungen die Büchermagazine untergebracht, in den oberirdischen »Steinquadern« die öffentlichen Bereiche sowie die Verwaltung. Die beiden oberirdischen Kuben sind mit mosaikartigen und effektvoll plastisch angeordneten Steinplatten verkleidet. Die aufhellende Glasur verhilft der Baumasse mit einer Nutzfläche von mehr als 30 000 Quadratmetern zu einer fast transparenten Leichtigkeit. Die streng angeordneten Kuben vermitteln dem Betrachter eine einfache Assoziation – die Vorstellung von riesigen Bücherregalen, wobei die scheinbar endlose Reihung von Buchrücken zu verschwimmen scheint.

Today's relentless growth in information, whether as books or sound and video recordings, requires up-to-date buildings where that information can be appropriately stored and accessed quickly. After the War, Saxony's State Library moved to Albertstadt into premises that now fall short of modern requirements. Since 2002, the Library, which includes rich holdings from the age of the Electors, has had a new home that it shares with the Library of Dresden's Technical University. They are now found on the campus at Zellescher Weg, an area where many of the institutes of the then Polytechnic were established after 1945. For functional reasons, Ortner & Ortner Architects chose to build both underground and above ground. Because many items are light sensitive and hugely valuable, the stacks are found in the secure underground section; the parts of the building above ground contain public areas and administrative offices. The two rectangular buildings above ground are clad in stone slabs with vertical banding. Standing looking at these two buildings facing each other across the reading room's glass ceiling, one is reminded of endless rows of books whose spines seem to blur. Altogether the building has more than 30,000 m² of usable space.

Die oberirdischen Verwaltungsgebäude der SLUB.
Administration offices in Saxony's State and University Library (SLUB).

Die Fassade des Südriegels spiegelt sich im Glasdach des Lesesaals.
The façade of the south building is reflected in the glass ceiling of the reading room.

Johannstadt mit Großem Garten, Gläserner Manufaktur und St. Benno-Gymnasium

Johannstadt and Grosser Garten, Transparent Factory and St. Benno Gymnasium

An der Nord-Westseite von Dresdens »Grüner Lunge«, dem Großen Garten, entstand die Gläserne Manufaktur von VW als Ausdruck für die Architektur des 21. Jahrhunderts. Das traditionelle Ausstellungsgelände war 1945 zerstört und danach abgerissen worden. In unattraktiven Nachkriegsprovisorien fanden verschiedene Ausstellungen statt, von der »Kunstausstellung« bis zur »Dresdener Vogelwiese«. Im Auftrag des Automobilherstellers Volkswagen schufen Gunter Henn Architekten & Ingenieure eine gläserne »Kathedrale des Hightech-Zeitalters«, in der Luxuswagen in Handarbeit entstehen. Der ausgedehnte Komplex zwischen Botanischem Garten der TU, Großem Garten und Straßburger Platz schafft fließende Übergänge zur Parklandschaft und behauptet sich selbstbewusst gegenüber den angrenzenden Wohnblöcken. Die symbolische Umsetzung von Erkennungsmerkmalen der Marke VW erfolgt in der architektonischen Auflockerung der Fassade im Eingangsbereich der Lennéstraße.

Im Park versteckt und im Schnittpunkt der beiden Hauptalleen verkörpert das restaurierte Palais im Großen Garten von Johann Georg Starcke aus dem 17. Jahrhundert den Durchbruch des Barock in Dresden, ohne ins Stadtzentrum einbezogen zu sein.

Kontroversen löste das neue St. Benno-Gymnasium (1994–96) in der Johannstadt aus. Vor allem die Abschirmung der Schule von der verkehrsreichen Güntzstraße durch eine blaue Wandscheibe und die terrassenförmige Gestaltung der Fassade auf der Rückseite sowie die ungewohnte Farbigkeit stießen auf Ablehnung. Inzwischen wird der von Günter Behnisch & Partner entwickelte Typus für ein modernes Gymnasium akzeptiert.

On the north-west edge of the Grosser Garten, Dresden's lungs, stands a striking example of twenty-first-century architecture, Volkswagen's Transparent Factory. The city's long-established exhibition centre had stood here until it was destroyed in 1945. Thereafter exhibitions and fairs continued to be held in unattractive makeshift structures. Commissioned by the German carmaker Volkswagen, the firm of Henn Architects & Engineers has created a transparent "cathedral to the age of hi-tech" in which luxury cars are hand-built. This is a large complex lying between the University's Botanical Garden and Strassburger Platz but the boundaries between it and the surrounding park dissolve and it sits comfortably beside the adjacent blocks of flats. The perceived characteristics of VW the Brand are symbolically realised in the softening of the design of the façade at the entrance on Lennéstrasse.

Hidden within the park and lying at the junction of its two main avenues, the now restored seventeenth-century château in the Grosser Garten by Johann Georg Starcke marks the breakthrough of the Baroque in Dresden.

The new St. Benno Gymnasium (1994–96) in the district of Johannstadt proved to be controversial. Its long blue wall shielding the school from the busy Güntzstrasse, its stepped terraces on the sculpted west façade and its unusually bright colours were found by some to be objectionable. This design for a contemporary school by Günter Behnisch & Partners has now become accepted. Johannstadt was the part of Dresden that suffered the most damage to its housing stock and cultural facilities on 13–14 February 1945.

Die Zeit entführt die Schönheit, Skulptur im Großen Garten, im Hintergrund das barocke Palais.
Time abducting Beauty: Sculpture in the Grosser Garten; in the background, Dresden's first baroque palace.

Fassadengestaltung des St. Benno-Gymnasiums.
The façade of St. Benno Gymnasium.

Innenbereich der Gläsernen Manufaktur.
Inside the Transparent Factory.

Die Gläserne Manufaktur am Rand des Großen Gartens.
The Transparent Factory at the edge of the Grosser Garten.

Dass dieses Palais einmal als Porzellanschloss für einen König gedacht war, der von sich sagte, er sei der »maladie de porcelaine« verfallen, gehört zu den wahren Geschichten, die sich um August den Starken ranken. Wenn sich sein Traum erfüllt hätte, wäre der pavillonartig geschwungene Dachaufbau Pöppelmanns heute nicht mit Kupfer, sondern mit Porzellanziegeln gedeckt. Das war jedoch auch damals nicht nur eine Frage der Finanzen, sondern vor allem der Technologie: weder Ziegel noch Großplastiken waren gegen Brandrisse gefeit. 1717 hatte August II. das am rechten Elbufer gelegene, damals Holländisches Palais genannte Gebäude erworben, um seine prächtige Sammlung chinesischer und japanischer Porzellane, ergänzt durch Arbeiten der Königlichen Manufaktur Meißen zu präsentieren. Bereits 1722 plante er das Palais, das für die stetig wachsende Sammlung »Weißen Goldes« bald zu klein geworden war, zu einem grandiosen Porzellanschloss zu erweitern. Ein Vorhaben, das auch unter seinem Nachfolger nicht ausgeführt wurde. Später zogen die Antikensammlung und die Landesbibliothek in die Räume ein. Heute teilen sich das Museum zur Sächsischen Vorgeschichte und das Völkerkundemuseum das Haus.

Der Blick geht über die Dachlandschaft mit den dreiachsigen Eckrisaliten in den Hof, dessen dreiseitiger Umgang von zwölf gewaltigen Japanerhermen getragen wird, eine Reminiszenz an die damalige orientalische Mode.

It is indeed true that the Japanese Palace was built to house the collection of porcelain belonging to Augustus the Strong, who himself claimed to suffer from *maladie de porcelaine*. If he had realised his dream, its sweeping roofs would now be covered in porcelain tiles rather than copper. At the time, it was not only a question of cost, but technology, too: neither glazed tiles nor statuary was immune to crazing. In 1717, the King acquired the building known at the time as the Dutch Palace on the right bank of the Elbe to allow him to display his magnificent collection of Chinese and Japanese porcelain that was augmented by pieces made for him at Meissen. It quickly became too small for his store of "white gold" and so as early as 1722, Augustus II drew up plans to convert it into an even grander home for his collection. The plan was not realised, however, even under his successor. The Antiquities' Collections, and later even the State Library, were instead housed in the building that is now home to Saxony's state museums of archaeology and ethnology.

The view of the curved pagoda roofs also shows the courtyard whose triangular ambulatory is supported by colossal statues that reveal the contemporary taste for oriental motifs.

Die Rähnitzgasse mit Blick auf den Turm der Dreikönigskirche.
The spire of the Church of the Epiphany as seen from Rähnitzgasse.

Oben: Die barocke Königstraße vom Palaisplatz in Richtung Norden, rechts der Turm der Dreikönigskirche.
Unten: Das Japanische Palais an der Großen Meißner Straße.
Top: Looking north along Baroque Königstrasse from Palaisplatz; the spire of the Church of the Epiphany is seen on the right.
Bottom: The Japanese Palace in Grosse Meissner Strasse.

Albertplatz mit Villa Eschebach

Albertplatz and Villa Eschebach

Am Bautzner Tor, dem heutigen Albertplatz, endete das rechtselbische mittelalterliche Dresden, präziser Altendresden, oder wie es ab dem 19. Jahrhundert hieß: die Neustadt. Nachdem die Festungsanlagen nach dem Abzug Napoleons abgetragen wurden, entstand an deren Stelle um 1817 eine klassizistische Rundplatzanlage, auf die sternförmig zwölf Straßen mündeten. Gottlob Friedrich Thormeyer gestaltete das Rondell, das trotz schwerer Kriegsverluste seine großstädtische Eleganz bewahren konnte. Die ausdrucksstarken Bronzefiguren von Robert Diez, die unter dem Wasserschleier lagern, gaben der 1893/94 von Clemens Grundig geschaffenen Doppelbrunnenanlage den Namen »Stilles Wasser« und »Stürmische Wogen«.

Verkörperte die Villa Eschebach noch den Reichtum des Küchenmöbel-Fabrikanten Carl Eschebach, der sich einen aufwendigen neobarocken Wohnsitz mit Palmenhaus inmitten der Stadt leisten konnte, so bieten die angrenzenden Plattenbauten aus DDR-Zeiten einen städtebaulichen Kontrast. Ohne ambitionierte Anbindung an gleichwertige Architektur wirkt der von Hans Erlwein 1906 als Tempietto gefasste Artesische Brunnen auf der Nordseite des Platzes verloren.

Als Musterbeispiel für gelungene Stadterneuerung kann die mit viel Liebe zum Detail sanierte barocke Königstraße gelten, die als breite Achse vom Albertplatz, vorbei an der Dreikönigskirche, zum Japanischen Palais führt. Die im Krieg stark zerstörte, ehemals barocke Hauptstraße verbindet den Albertplatz mit dem Neustädter Markt, wo der »Goldene Reiter« – ein 1736 geschaffenes Reiterdenkmal Augusts des Starken – an die historische »Neue Königsstadt« erinnert.

Medieval Dresden north of the Elbe, or to be more precise Altendresden, ended at Bautzner Tor, today's Albertplatz. After the nineteenth century, the area was called Neustadt. Following Napoleon's departure, its fortifications were razed and just there, around 1817, a neoclassical circus was laid out with twelve streets leading off. Designed by Gottlob Friedrich Thormeyer, it has preserved its aura of metropolitan elegance despite severe wartime losses. Robert Diez's expressive, water-swept bronze sculptures lent the two fountains, the work of Clemens Grundig in 1893–94, the name of *Still Water and Stormy Waves*. The Villa Eschebach (now a bank) epitomizes the wealth of Carl Eschebach, a manufacturer of kitchen furniture who could well afford to build a lavish, neo-baroque town house complete with palm house. The adjacent prefabs from G.D.R. days form something of a stylistic contrast. Hans Erlwein's 1906 tempietto-like artesian well on the north side of the square now appears lost in its setting.

Forming a wide avenue from Albertplatz, going past the Dreikönigskirche (Church of the Epiphany), and leading to the Japanese Palace, baroque Königstrasse is a model of successful and painstaking urban renewal. Hauptstrasse, also once known for its baroque buildings, was badly damaged in the war. It connects Albertplatz and Neustädter Markt, where the Golden Horseman, an equestrian statue of Augustus the Strong dating from 1736, is reminiscent of the historical "Neue Königsstadt" and long a symbol of the city.

Blick über den Albertplatz mit den beiden Brunnenanlagen »Stilles Wasser« und »Stürmische Wogen«, Vorkriegsaufnahme.
Pre-war photograph of the Albertplatz showing the fountains known as "Still Water" and "Stormy Waves".

Schmiedeeisernes Torgitter am Eingang zur Villa Eschebach.
Wrought-iron gate at the entrance to Villa Eschebach.

Haupteingang und ehemaliges Palmenhaus der Villa Eschebach.
Villa Eschebach: main entrance and former palm house.

Äußere Neustadt

Die äußere Neustadt ist das größte, noch erhaltene Gründerzeitviertel Deutschlands. Sein heutiges Gesicht bekam der Stadtteil, der sich zwischen Königsbrücker und Bautzner Straße erstreckt, kurz vor dem Ausgang des 19. Jahrhunderts. Historismus und vereinzelt Jugendstil lagen dicht beieinander, in den Hinterhöfen der großen Mietshäuser drängten sich bescheidene Wohnhäuser und kleine Fabriken von Gewerbetreibenden. Im Schatten der Königsbrücker Straße wuchs der Schriftsteller Erich Kästner auf, der diesem Viertel mit seinen Kindheitserinnerungen *Als ich ein kleiner Junge war* ein Denkmal gesetzt hat. Das pulsierende Leben der »Bunten Republik Neustadt« zeigt sich vor allem in der Kneipen- und Kleinkunstszene, die sich trotz aller notwendigen Modernisierungen der verfallenen Hinterhöfe erfolgreich behauptet. Zahlreiche Einzelhändler haben sich hier mit Boutiquen, Buchläden und Ateliers eine Existenz aufgebaut. Sehenswert ist die Kunsthofpassage zwischen Alaun- und Görlitzer Straße – Anziehungspunkt für Einheimische und Touristen gleichermaßen. Der älteste jüdische Friedhof Dresdens im Martin-Luther-Viertel, das mit EU-Hilfe aufwändig sanierte Nordbad sowie Ballsäle, Kinos und die berühmte Molkerei der Gebrüder Pfund schaffen ein Kolorit, das sich wohltuend von uniformer Stadtgestaltung abhebt. Industriell montierte Kinderspielanlagen sucht man hier vergebens, stattdessen haben sich die Bewohner, eine bunte Mischung aus Jung und Alt, Einheimischen und Zugezogenen, kleine grüne Inseln im Häusermeer geschaffen. Auch ausländische Besucher können sich hier seit jeher heimisch fühlen. Das lobte schon der polnische Romancier Josef Ignacy Kraszewski, der über zwanzig Jahre in Dresden lebte, u.a. in einem Landhaus in der Nordstraße 28, das heute Museum ist.

Äussere Neustadt

The district of Äussere Neustadt is the largest remaining example in Germany of urban development from the time of the country's rapid industrial expansion. Lying between Königsbrücker Strasse and Bautzner Strasse, this part of town owes its appearance to the end of the nineteenth century. Buildings imitating past styles and the occasional example of Jugendstil were found here; modest dwellings and tradesmen's workshops were squeezed into the courtyards of large apartment blocks. The author Erich Kästner grew up a stone's throw from Königsbrücker Strasse. Through his childhood memoirs, *When I was a Little Boy*, the district lives on. Known locally as the "Colourful Republic of Neustadt", this is a happening place with a lively pub and cabaret scene that is managing to survive despite the necessary refurbishment of the dilapidated backyards it calls home. Numerous people now make their living here in boutiques, bookstores and studios. Well worth seeing is the Kunsthofpassage between Alaun- and Görlitzer Strasse – it attracts locals and tourists alike. The oldest Jewish cemetery in the city in the Martin Luther Quarter, the Nordbad (extensively refurbished with European Union funds), plus dancehalls, cinemas and the famous dairy that belonged to the Pfund brothers all add to the atmosphere here that forms a pleasant contrast to the uniformity normally associated with town planning. Don't look for mass-produced children's playgrounds here. Instead the colourful mix of young and old, locals and newcomers, have created their own small green oases among the surrounding mass of houses. Foreign visitors, too, have felt at home here, and not just recent ones either. The Polish novelist Josef Ignacy Kraszewski sang the praises of this part of Dresden where he lived for over twenty years including, among other places, a cottage at 28 Nordstrasse which now houses a museum to him.

Die Rothenburger Straße.
Rothenburger street.

Fassade im »Hof der Elemente« in der Kunsthofpassage.
The façade of the "Courtyard of the Elements" in the Kunsthofpassage.

Links: Fenstergestaltung in der Böhmischen Straße.
Rechts: Innenhof des Café Raskolnikoff.
Left: Windows in Böhmische Strasse.
Right: The courtyard of Café Raskolnikoff.

Albertstadt und Garnisonskirche

Neben Potsdam gehörte das Ende des 19. Jahrhunderts planmäßig am Hellerhang angelegte Militärviertel zu den seinerzeit modernsten Garnisonsstädten des Deutschen Reiches. Benannt nach König Albert von Sachsen, expandierte die Kasernenstadt mit einer vorzüglichen Infrastruktur beiderseits einer 3 Kilometer langen und bis zu 30 Meter breiten Heeresstraße, die heute Stauffenberg-Allee heißt. Ein wechselvolles, steingewordenes Kapitel deutscher Militärgeschichte, schwer gezeichnet vom Zerfall. Wo einst sächsische Regimenter mit klingendem Spiel ins Manöver und zu Paraden ausrückten, erinnern nur noch Namen wie »Heeresbäckerei« an die Garnisonsstadt, in der bis zu 20 000 Soldaten lebten. Den königlichen Regimentern folgten Reichswehr und Wehrmacht. Nach dem Krieg bezog die Rote Armee viele der Kasernen. Das ehemalige Königlich-Sächsische Arsenal (nach 1945 Stadthalle) gibt als Militärhistorisches Museum einen Überblick über die sächsisch-deutsche Militärgeschichte vom Mittelalter bis zur Gegenwart. Viele der Kasernen und Lazarette werden als Verwaltungsgebäude (Regierungspräsidium an der Stauffenberg-Allee) oder Schulen, wie die Heeresoffiziersschule der Bundeswehr genutzt. Solide Gründerzeitarchitektur rief weitsichtige Investoren auf den Plan. In der Pionierkaserne an der Königsbrücker Straße, in der einst Erich Kästner diente, befindet sich nach Umbau unter denkmalschützerischen Vorgaben das Landesfunkhaus des Mitteldeutschen Rundfunks. Von Lossow & Viehweger stammt die byzantinische wie romanische Elemente vereinende Garnisonskirche. 1893 bis 1900 als Simultankirche für den evangelischen und katholischen Gottesdienst errichtet, dient sie heute kulturellen wie kirchlichen Zwecken.

Taking its name from King Albert of Saxony, the Albertstadt Garrison, alongside Potsdam, was the most modern in Germany when it was built from 1873–80. With excellent infrastructure, this garrison town extended for three kilometres (1.86 miles) along both sides of a military road that measured up to 30 metres (32 yards) wide. Today, it is called Stauffenberg Allee in honour of the general staff officer executed for his part in the July 1944 plot against Hitler. The complex has seen the highs and lows of German military history and is now in a sad state of repair. Where Saxony's regiments once paraded or set out on manoeuvres to the sound of military bands, nowadays only names like Heeresbäckerei (army bakery) are reminders of the garrison town that held up to 20,000 men. The royal Saxon regiments were followed by the Reichswehr (1919–35) and the Wehrmacht (1935–45). The Red Army commandeered many of the barracks after World War II. What used to be the Royal Saxon Arsenal now houses a museum examining Saxon and German military history from the Middle Ages to the present. Many of the barracks and hospitals are now used by the German army, including its Officers' School. Local author Erich Kästner once served in the Pioneer Barracks on Königsbrücker Strasse; after carefully controlled refurbishment, they now house the headquarters of the regional radio station, MDR. Lossow & Viehweger designed the Garrison Church with its Byzantine elements on a Romanesque plan. Built from 1893 to 1900, both Protestant and Catholic services were held in it; nowadays it is used for church services and cultural events.

Eines der wichtigsten Bauwerke der Albertstadt ist das ehemalige Arsenal von 1874–75.
One of the most important buildings of Albertstadt is the former arsenal from 1874–75.

Die malerische Garnisonskirche vereint zwei Konfessionen unter ihrem Dach.
The picturesque Garnisonskirche houses two denominations under one roof.

Hellerau – die Gartenstadt

Die Gartenstadt Hellerau im Norden Dresdens entstand vor dem Ersten Weltkrieg. Mit sozialreformerischer Absicht begründete Karl Schmidt 1907 die »Deutschen Werkstätten für Handwerkskunst«, eine Anlage, die sich mit den dazugehörigen Eigenheimsiedlungen an das in England entwickelte Modell einer Gartenstadt anlehnt. Die Gestaltung der Straßenzeilen und Plätze im Einklang mit den Werkstätten harmoniert mit der ländlichen Atmosphäre, die der lebensreformerischen Forderung nach gesunden Arbeits- und Lebensbedingungen entsprach. Den Architekten Richard Riemerschmid und Hermann Muthesius sind Haustypen zu verdanken, die auf Zweckmäßigkeit und Schönheit, bis hin zur Innenausstattung mit industriell gefertigten Möbeln, ausgerichtet waren, die sich auch Arbeiter leisten konnten. Unterstützt von Wolf Dohrn, dem Geschäftsführer der Gartenstadtgesellschaft, gründete der Schweizer Pädagoge Emile Jaques Dalcroze eine Bildungsanstalt für rhythmischen Tanz, die 1911 im Festspielhaus von Heinrich Tessenow eine Heimstatt fand. Der symmetrisch angelegte und sich am Neoklassizismus orientierende Bau fällt durch seinen hohen Säulenportikus auf, während die beiden Seitenflügel sich dem Mittelbau unterordnen. Aufsehen erregte die Saalarchitektur, die erstmals ohne Bühne den Rahmen für weitgreifende Licht-Klang- und Rauminstallationen abgab. Für kurze Zeit war Hellerau eine internationale Künstlerkolonie: George Bernhard Shaw, Paul Claudel, Franz Kafka, Max Reinhardt, Mary Wigman und andere europäische Intellektuelle fühlten sich angezogen. Der Faschismus beendete den Aufbruch in die Moderne endgültig. Das Festspielgelände wurde als Kaserne zweckentfremdet. In der Gegenwart ist man bemüht, verschiedene Institutionen, z.B. den Werkbund und das Zentrum für zeitgenössische Musik, in Hellerau zu etablieren.

Hellerau – The Garden City

The town of Hellerau, in the north of Dresden, was established by Karl Schmidt in 1907 along the lines of the English 'garden city'. Schmidt founded the Deutsche Werkstätten für Handwerkskunst (German Artisans' Workshops) and also provided homes for the people working there. The colony's streets and square blend harmoniously with the workshops and the natural surroundings, and are an expression of the founder's belief in healthy living and working conditions. The architects Richard Riemerschmid and Hermann Muthesius designed houses characterized by functionality and beauty; they were furnished with mass-produced goods that workers could afford to buy. With the support of Wolf Dohrn, the company's managing director, the Swiss teacher Émile Jaques-Dalcroze in 1911 established an Institute of Eurhythmics that found a home in Heinrich Tessenow's Festival Theatre, a symmetrical, neoclassical building with a striking portico flanked by two smaller wings. Its auditorium was a talking point: it had no proscenium arch or raised stage, but instead an open performance space with no barrier between the performers and the audience. Innovative and influential light and sound performances were staged there. For a short while, Hellerau was home to a colony of writers and artists, among them George Bernhard Shaw, Paul Claudel, Franz Kafka, Max Reinhardt and Mary Wigman as well as other European intellectuals. The rise of the Nazis finally put a stop to Hellerau's progressive approach and later the colony became a barracks. Efforts are now being directed towards establishing various institutions here, for instance a latter-day Werkbund and a Centre of Contemporary Music.

Die Deutschen Werkstätten Hellerau.
Hellerau, the "Deutsche Werkstätten".

Reihenhäuser von Richard Riemerschmid.
Terraced housing by Richard Riemerschmid.

Säulenportal des Hellerauer Festspielhauses von Heinrich Tessenow.
The portico of Heinrich Tessenow's Festival Theatre at Hellerau.

Seit einigen Jahren kann man wieder im Ballhaus Watzke am Pieschener Hafen einkehren, bei schönem Wetter im Biergarten sitzen und den Blick auf die Dresdener Silhouette genießen. Um die Jahrhundertwende gab es über 150 ähnliche Vergnügungsetablissements in der Stadt. Gemeinsam war ihnen die Innenausstattung mit einem großen Tanzsaal mit Konzertmuschel und die auf gusseisernen Säulen ruhende Galerie. Prächtige Deckenmalereien und große Leuchter steigerten den festlichen Eindruck. Benno Hübel baute 1898/99 für den Gastwirt Watzke dieses zweigeschossige Ballhaus mit Restaurant im unteren und zweistöckigem Saal im Obergeschoss. Die Schaufassade zur Straße besteht aus Klinkern, der Treppenturm an der linken Seite schafft den Ausgleich zum Saalgiebel, der in Neorenaissanceformen schwelgt. Vorbei die tristen Zeiten, in denen eines der schönsten Ballhäuser – entlang der Elbe gab es eine ganze »Ballhausmeile« – als Großlager für Sportartikel der volkseigenen HO (Handelsorganisation) diente, um irgendwann vom Abriss ereilt zu werden. Pieschen entwickelte sich bis zum Beginn des 20. Jahrhunderts, gemeinsam mit den Vororten Mickten, Trachau und Kaditz, zum Industrie- und Gewerbestandort, bewohnt von Fabrikanten, Arbeitern und Angestellten. Den gesellschaftlichen Bedürfnissen entsprechend wurden Mietshäuser gebaut, deren Fassaden sparsam dekoriert waren. Die Tendenz zum funktionalen Bauen gegenüber der stilistisch überladenen Villenarchitektur dominierte. Belege dafür finden sich beispielsweise an der Leipziger Straße: Schilling & Graebners Doppelhaus für den Dresdener Spar- und Bauverein von 1901/02. Eine mustergültige Fabrikanlage stellen die ehemaligen Eschebachschen Werke an der Riesaer Straße dar. Die roten Backsteinbauten wurden nach 1989 umgebaut und werden jetzt von verschiedenen städtischen Ämtern genutzt.

For some years now, it has again been possible to stop off at Watzke's Ballroom at Pieschen harbour to enjoy a drink in the beer garden and take in the view of Dresden. Around 1900, the city had over 150 such venues. They all had a large ballroom with a recessed stage for the orchestra and a gallery supported by cast-iron pillars. Splendid painted ceilings and large chandeliers further enhanced the sense of opulence. Built in 1898–99, this two-storey building with its downstairs restaurant and upstairs ballroom on two levels was designed by Benno Hübel. Its decorative façade uses clinker bricks, while the stair tower on the left offsets the high ballroom gable that revels in Neo-Renaissance themes. Gone now are the days when one of the city's loveliest ballrooms – one of many beside the river – was used as a warehouse for sports goods sold by the H.O., the State Retail Store in the G.D.R., and was threatened with demolition. By the beginning of the twentieth century, Pieschen, along with the suburbs of Mickten, Trachau and Kaditz, had developed into an industrial and business centre where manufacturers and factory and office workers lived. To house everybody, sparse-looking apartment blocks were built. Here functionalism took precedence over the stylistic excesses of the city's villas. An example of such functionalism can be seen in Leipziger Strasse in the form of Schilling & Graebner's semi-detached house that was built in 1901–02 for the Dresden Savings Bank. Eschebach's Factory on Riesaer Strasse is a fine example of industrial building. It was converted after 1989 and now houses a number of local government offices.

Typische Eckbebauung der Gründerzeit an der Leipziger Straße.
Typical corner building from the late nineteenth century on Leipziger Strasse.

Ballhaus Watzke, Straßenansicht.
Watzke's Ballroom as seen from the street.

Innenhof der ehemaligen Eschebachschen Werke.
Internal courtyard of the former Eschebach Works.

Friedrichstadt und Ostragehege

Friedrichstadt and Ostragehege

Die barocke Bauphase der Friedrichstadt lässt sich am Komplex des Krankenhauses (Marcolini-Palais), einigen restaurierten Häusern in der Friedrichstraße sowie der Matthäuskirche von Matthäus Daniel Pöppelmann erkennen. Der Stadtteil öffnet sich nach der Elbe durch die Anbindung an den Alberthafen und das Ostragehege. Am Südkai ragt der von Kühne und Lossow gebaute Siloturm der Hafenmühle in den Himmel, 1913 als eine der größten deutschen Getreidemühlen im Auftrag der Firma Bienert (Brotbäckerei) fertig gestellt. Aus Rentabilitätsgründen wurde das Hafenbecken in den neunziger Jahren verkleinert. Auf dem weiträumigen Areal des Ostrageheges ließ die Stadt 1910 durch den Stadtbaurat Hans Erlwein den zentralen Vieh- und Schlachthof errichten, dessen markantester Punkt der massige Kühlturm ist. Nachdem die Fleischverarbeitung nach 1990 eingestellt wurde, hat man einige der historisch bedeutenden Bauten in das Ausstellungskonzept der »Neuen Messe« einbezogen. Die Erweiterung von Sport- und Freizeitanlagen in der reizvollen Elbaue ist zukünftig vorgesehen, nicht zuletzt deshalb, weil die bereits im 18. Jahrhundert geplante städtebauliche Achse auf Schloss Übigau ausgerichtet ist.

Das 1724–26 als einziges Dresdener Bauwerk von Eosander von Göthe errichtete Schloss gehörte einst zu der von August dem Starken geplanten Bebauung der Elbufer nach dem Vorbild des venezianischen Ganal Grande. Während das elbaufwärts gelegene Lustschloss Pillnitz zu den meistbesuchten Dresdener Sehenswürdigkeiten gehört, steht Schloss Übigau heute nach jahrzehntelanger Vernachlässigung leer.

The hospital (Marcolini Palace), some refurbished houses in Friedrichstrasse as well as Pöppelmann's Church of St. Matthew (Matthäuskirche) are examples of baroque architecture in this part of the city. In 1910, Ostragehege was chosen as the location for the main cattle market and slaughterhouse with its striking cooling tower. Hans Erlwein, the city's architect, built the complex that lent its name to a novel, *Slaughterhouse Five*, by the American author Kurt Vonnegut. Built in 1913 by Kühne and Lossow, the silo belonged to one of Germany's largest flour mill towers over the dock's south quay. In 1990, the harbour basin was reduced in size as a cost-saving measure. When meat processing ended after 1990, some of the architecturally significant buildings here were incorporated into the Neue Messe, Dresden's exhibition centre. In future, it is planned to extend the sports and other recreational facilities in this attractive riverside setting, not least because of the view across to Übigau Palace that as early as the eighteenth century was the focus of architects' plans.

The only building in Dresden by Eosander von Göthe, Übigau was built from 1724–26 and was part of a scheme by Augustus the Strong to develop the banks of the Elbe along the lines of the Grand Canal in Venice. While Pillnitz Palace further upstream is one of the most visited attractions in Dresden, Übigau Palace has suffered decades of neglect and is now empty.

Matthäuskirche von Matthäus Daniel Pöppelmann.
Matthäus Daniel Pöppelmann's Church of St. Matthew.

Der Alberthafen.
The Albert Dock.

Die Hafenmühle wurde wegen des weithin sichtbaren Siloturms
»Getreidekirche« genannt.
The riverside mill was known as the "Grain Church" because of
its silo that was visible from afar.

Glaskonstruktionen und Naturstein verbinden auf dem neuen Messegelände am alten Schlachthof moderne Messebauten mit Jugendstilarchitektur.
At the new exhibition centre on the former site of the slaughterhouse, glass and stone forge links between contemporary buildings and "Jugendstil" architecture.

Ehemaliges Tabakkontor Yenidze

The Former Yenidze Tobacco and Cigarette Factory

Wie eine Moschee ragt das ehemalige Tabakkontor »Yenidze« am Rande der Friedrichstadt empor. Der Industriebau wurde 1907 bis 1912 von Hermann Martin Hammitzsch im Auftrag des Zigarettenfabrikanten Hugo Zietz errichtet.

Für diesen Produktionsbau im pseudo-orientalischen Stil nach maurisch-mameluckischem Vorbild, der völlig aus dem Rahmen Dresdener Bautradition fiel, wurde der Baumeister aus der Architektenkammer ausgeschlossen. Der originelle Stahlbeton-Skelettbau – einer der ersten in Deutschland – mit der von innen beleuchteten 18 Meter hohen Glaskuppel und den als Minaretten drapierten Schornsteinen und Belüftungsschächten wird heute vielfältig als Bürohaus, Restaurant und Diskothek genutzt. Kachelmosaike in den Eingangsbereichen und die durchbrochenen Zinnen aus Werkstein im gesamten Traufbereich betonen den orientalischen Charakter des Werksgebäudes, das gleichzeitig eine überdimensionale, weithin sichtbare Werbefläche war. »Orientalische Tabak- und Zigarettenfabrik Yenidze« lautete der Firmenname, der sich auf das Anbaugebiet um die türkische Stadt Yenidze bezieht. 1945 war auch dieses monumentale Bauwerk infolge der Bombardierungen schwer beschädigt. Die wiedererrichtete, farbig verglaste Kuppel ist heute beliebter Veranstaltungsort für »orientalische« Märchenlesungen.

Looking like a mosque, Yenidze towers into the air at the edge of the district of Friedrichstadt. Hermann Martin Hammitzsch built this former factory from 1907–12 for the cigarette manufacturer Hugo Zietz. With its pseudo-oriental style along Moorish-Mameluke lines, this building was wholly unlike anything previously built in the city – and its architect was expelled from his professional association because of it! The reinforced concrete skeleton – one of the first in Germany – is topped by an 18-metre-high glass dome that is illuminated from within at night; its chimneys and ventilation shafts were disguised as minarets. The tiles in the entrance and the crenelated balustrade at roof height emphasize the exotic character of the building that was visible from afar and was, in fact, a monumental advertisement for Zietz's products. The company's name was Oriental Tobacco and Cigarette Factory Yenidze in reference to the Turkish city of Yenidze from where it sourced its raw material. The building was badly damaged in 1945. Nowadays it contains offices, restaurants and a club and the coloured glass dome has become a popular venue for readings of "oriental" fairy tales.

Die gläserne Kuppel orientiert sich an ägyptischen Mameluckengräbern.
The glass dome is based on Egyptian Mameluke graves.

Das ehemalige Tabakkontor zwischen Bahndamm und Ostragehege.
The former building for the cigarette manufacturer between Bahndamm and Ostrahege.

Ernemann-Bau in Striesen

Das ehemalige Produktionsgebäude der Ernemann Werke AG an der Schandauer/Junghansstraße im Stadtteil Striesen gehört zu den markanten Industriebauten des 20. Jahrhunderts. Der zunächst vierflügelige Bau in Eisenbeton-Skelettbauweise (1915–1918 ausgeführt) wurde Anfang der zwanziger Jahre durch ein zwölfgeschossiges Turmhaus für repräsentative Verwaltungsräume und ein Planetarium (Höhe 48 Meter) ergänzt. Den Grundstock für dieses Zentrum der heimischen Fotoindustrie legte Friedrich Enzmann, der bereits 1839 Kameras und Fotoplatten herstellte. Um 1900 waren die von Johann Heinrich Ernemann gegründeten Werke führend in der Herstellung von Kameras. Zwanzig Jahre später wurde daraus die Ernemann-Krupp-Kinoapparate-GmbH, die sich zum Unternehmen Zeiss-Ikon ausweitete. 1936 wurde die erste einäugige Kleinbild-Spiegelreflexkamera der Welt in Dresden entwickelt. Mit dem Umzug des größten deutschen Fotopapierherstellers, der Mimosa AG, von Köln in die nahegelegene Bärensteiner Straße erweiterte sich das Industriezentrum auf dem Striesener und Blasewitzer Areal. Eine auch heute noch erkennbare hervorragende Infrastruktur war typisch für diese Mischung von Wohn- und Industriegebiet, wie sie außerhalb der historischen Stadtmitte anzutreffen war. Im Zweiten Weltkrieg wurden einige der Werke zerstört. Fünf der Kamerabetriebe, die in der DDR enteignet wurden, schlossen sich zum VEB Pentacon (Volkseigener Betrieb) zusammen, der weiterhin Spielreflexkameras der Praktica-Reihe produzierte. Nach 1989 erlosch dieser Industriezweig bis auf wenige Ausnahmen. Im Ernemann-Bau sind heute die technischen Sammlungen untergebracht, die zusammen mit der Hermann-Krone-Sammlung der TU an eine große Tradition erinnern.

Ernemann-Bau at Striesen

The former manufacturing plant of Ernemann Werke AG on the corner of Schandauer Strasse and Junghans Strasse in the district of Striesen is among the twentieth century's notable industrial buildings. Built between 1915–18 as a reinforced concrete skeleton structure with four wings, it was extended at the beginning of the 1920s with a twelve-storey tower to provide representative offices and a planetarium 48 metres in height. Friedrich Enzmann laid the foundations for the manufacture of photographic equipment in Saxony; his company was producing cameras and photographic plates as early as 1839. Around 1900, Johann Heinrich Ernemann's factory was a leader in camera manufacture. Twenty years later, the Ernemann-Krupp-Kinoapparate-GmbH was established to make motion picture cameras; it later grew into Zeiss-Ikon. The industrial area in Striesen and Blasewitz expanded when Mimosa AG, the largest German producer of photographic paper, moved from Cologne to Dresden's Bärensteiner Strasse. An excellent infrastructure, one that is apparent to this day, was typical of the combination of residential and industrial use that was found beyond the historic city centre. A number of the factories were destroyed in World War II. Five of the camera factories, expropriated in the G.D.R., merged to form Pentacon, a publicly owned firm that continued to produce Praktica reflex cameras. With few exceptions, the industry ceased to exist after 1989. Today the Ernemann-Bau is home to the Technical University's various technological collections, including the Hermann-Krone photographic collection that acts as a reminder of the city's great photographic tradition which, for instance, saw the development of the world's first 35-mm single-lens reflex camera in the city in 1936.

Der Turm des Ernemann-Baus war das Firmensignet der Pentacon-Werke.
The tower of the Ernemann-Bau was the logo for Pentacon.

Der Turmbau der ehemaligen Ernemann-Werke war ursprünglich als Sternwarte geplant.
The tower of the former Ernemann Works was originally planned as an observatory.

Blasewitzer Villen

Villas of Blasewitz

Blasewitz legte am Ausgang des 19. Jahrhunderts seinen dörflichen Charakter weitgehend ab. Anstelle niedriger Fachwerkhäuser breiteten sich herrschaftliche Villen aus. An Plätzen und Hauptstraßen konzentrierten sich Mietshäuser mit prächtiger Gründerzeitarchitektur. Blaswitz gehörte schon damals zu den teuersten Wohngegenden und wurde erst 1921 nach Dresden eingemeindet. Am Blasewitzer Rathaus steht die Figur der Gustel von Blasewitz. Der Dichter Friedrich Schiller hatte während eines Aufenthalts bei seinem Freund Gottfried Körner Gefallen an der Schankwirtstochter gefunden und Jahre später verarbeitete er seine Erinnerung, in dem er Justine Kerner in seinem Schauspiel *Wallenstein* eine literarische Episode widmete. Namhafte Dresdener Architekten wie Karl Emil Scherz und Martin Pietzsch verwirklichten hier im Auftrag vermögender Persönlichkeiten phantastische Villen in buntem Stilgemisch. Auch Dichter wie Gerhart Hauptmann oder Komponisten wie Sergej Rachmaninow bezogen gern eine der exklusiven Villen, von denen die meisten vom Bombenhagel im Februar 1945 verschont blieben. 1894/95 baute der Architekt Max Georg Poscharsky im Zwickel zwischen Goetheallee und heutigem Käthe-Kollwitz-Ufer einen Sommersitz, der sich in der Giebelgestaltung an die deutsche Renaissance anlehnt. Unterschiedliche Fensterformen, Erker, Türme und Loggien sowie Putzmalereien belegen die hohe technische Qualität damaliger Handwerkskunst. Die noble Innenausstattung mit Holzvertäfelungen und Stuckarbeiten in Jugendstil-Ornamentik wurde vollständig restauriert. Heute ist die Villa Weigang als Blasewitzer Standesamt öffentlich zugänglich und gewährt Einblick in die großbürgerliche Wohnkultur um 1900.

Blasewitz to a great extent lost its village quality at the end of the nineteenth century when low half-timbered houses were replaced by grand villas and apartment houses on its squares and main roads. Although it did not become part of Dresden until 1921, Blasewitz was one of the most desirable and expensive residential areas even then. In a mix of styles, renowned Dresden architects like Karl Emil Scherz and Martin Pietzsch created extravagant villas here for their affluent clients. Among those who lived in Blasewitz were the German playwright and novelist Gerhart Hauptmann and Russian composer Sergey Rachmaninoff. Fortunately, the area was hardly damaged in 1945. In 1894–95, the architect Max Georg Poscharsky built a summerhouse wedged between Goetheallee and today's Käthe-Kollwitz-Ufer. With gables modeled on the German Renaissance, it has a variety of window shapes, turrets, towers, loggias and external ornamentation that all testify to the great skill of the craftsmen of the day. The rich interior work includes wooden paneling and plasterwork using Jugendstil motifs. Now fully refurbished, the Villa Weigang at 55 Goetheallee is the local registry office and is open to the public. It offers interesting insights into upper class living around 1900.

Schmuckrelief an einem Torbogen, Goetheallee.
Ornamentation on an arched entrance, Goetheallee.

Glasfenster mit Jugenstilornamenten, Villa Weigang.
"Jugendstil" windows in the Villa Weigang.

Die Villa ist von einem großzügigen Gartenareal mit altem Baumbestand umgeben.
The Villa is surrounded by a spacious garden with mature trees.

Blaues Wunder und Loschwitzer Hang

Blaues Wunder and Loschwitz Heights

Das wegen seines Anstrichs so genannte Blaue Wunder gehört zu den auffälligsten technischen Denkmalen der Ingenieurbaukunst am Ende des 19. Jahrhunderts. Die Anklänge zum Pariser Eiffelturm sind trotz geringeren Ausmaßes (Spannweite 141, 5 Meter) unverkennbar. Die komplizierte Stahlwerkkonstruktion, von Claus Köpcke und Hans Manfred Krüger in nur zwei Jahren ab 1891 errichtet, kommt ohne Strompfeiler aus und verbindet die Ortsteile Blasewitz und Loschwitz. Ganz in der Nähe überwinden die Schwebeseilbahn (1898–1901) als erste in Europa und die Standseilbahn (1894/95) am Loschwitzer Hang einen Höhenunterschied von knapp 100 Meter auf einer Länge von einem halben Kilometer. Per Gondel oder mit dem Wagen gelangt man vom Körnerplatz zum Villenviertel auf den Weißen Hirsch und nach Oberloschwitz. Berg- und Talstationen wurden im historisierenden Stil ausgeführt. So wird zum Beispiel die ehemalige Maschinenstation der Schwebebahn in Oberloschwitz von einem trutzigen Bergfried verkleidet. Das geruhsame Verkehrstempo der beiden Bahnen lässt Nostalgie aufkommen. Im Dreigespann der Oldies fehlt allerdings seit 1986 die Straßenbahn, die einst über das Blaue Wunder entlang des Wachwitzer Elbhangs, vorbei an lauschig gelegenen Gartenrestaurants, bis zum Pillnitzer Schloss fuhr.

Taking its name from the colour of its paint, the Blaues Wunder (Blue Wonder) is one of the great German monuments to civil engineering of the late nineteenth century and is one of the country's most famous bridges. Even with a span of only 141.5 metres, it is still reminiscent of the Eiffel Tower. Construction work on Claus Köpcke's and Hans Manfred Krüger's complicated structure began in 1891 and was completed two years later; a steel suspension bridge, it links the villa suburbs of Blasewitz and Loschwitz. A hanging mountain railway (1898–1901, Europe's first) and a funicular railway (1894/95) are a short distance away; over a distance of 500 metres, they ascend almost 100 metres to the top of the Loschwitz Heights to marvel at the villas of Weisser Hirsch and Oberloschwitz. Following extensive refurbishment, now only passengers are carried. In their design, the stations looked to the past; for instance, at Oberloschwitz, a defiant donjon conceals the hanging railway's former powerhouse with its chimneys that were in use before the advent of electric motors. The leisurely pace of these old railways allows travellers to indulge in a little nostalgia. The tram that once crossed the Blue Wonder on its way to Pillnitz along the river past quiet inns unfortunately stopped running in 1986.

Das Blaue Wunder im Bau, historische Aufnahme von August Kotzsch, 1892.
The Blaues Wunder being built, historical photograph by August Kotzsch, 1892.

Eine Gondel der Schwebebahn in Fahrt über den Loschwitzer Hang.
A carriage of the suspended railway above the Loschwitz Heights.

Das Blaue Wunder hieß ursprünglich »König-Albert-Brücke« und
erhielt seinen Spitznamen durch den ungewöhnlichen Anstrich.
The Blaues Wunder was known originally as the King Albert Bridge
and owes its nickname to the unusual colour of its paint.

Elbhangschlösser

Hillside Villas overlooking the Elbe

Die Hanglage über der Elbe fand bereits Lord Findlater aus Schottland so reizvoll, dass er zu Beginn des 19. Jahrhunderts einige der alten Weinberge erwarb und darauf ein ansehnliches Palais errichten ließ. Begeistert von dem Ort zeigte sich auch Preußenprinz Albrecht, der Bruder des deutschen Kaisers Wilhelm I. Seinen Ansprüchen genügte Findlaters Landschloss jedoch nicht. Deshalb beauftragte er Adolph Lohse, einen Schinkelschüler, über den Gartenterrassen ein spätklassizistisches Schloss zu bauen, das äußerlich einer italienischen Renaissancevilla gleicht. Parallel entstand die benachbarte Villa Stockhausen für den Kammerherrn des Prinzen, die auch unter dem Namen des späteren Besitzers als Lingnerschloss bekannt wurde. Karl August Lingner, der Odol-Fabrikant und Begründer des Hygienemuseums, verfügte in seinem Testament die öffentliche Nutzung. Im terrassierten Weinberg fand er im Mausoleum von Hans Poelzig seine letzte Ruhestätte. Leider ist es um den städtischen Besitz noch nicht zum Besten bestellt. Als drittes der Elbhangschlösser prangt Schloss Eckberg wie ein kostbares Schmuckstück am grünen Hang, einst als Villa Souchay bekannt. Auf dem Bergvorsprung zwischen Mordgrund und Elbe errichtete Christian Friedrich Arnold den Sandsteinbau zwischen 1859 und 1861 für den englischen Großkaufmann John Daniel Souchay. Die im neugotischen Stil erbaute Villa gilt als Meisterwerk des Semperschülers. Einzigartig passt sich die Gartenanlage dem herrschaftlichen Anwesen an, in dem spätromantische Einflüsse nachklingen. Heute ist Schloss Eckberg ein exklusives Hotel, in dem auch Staatsgäste gern übernachten.

The Scots nobleman Lord Findlater was so charmed by the hillsides overlooking the river Elbe that he purchased some of the vineyards along their slopes and had a handsome villa built for himself at the beginning of the nineteenth century. Someone else who was inspired by the location was the Prussian Prince Albrecht, the brother of Kaiser William I. As Findlater's villa did not meet his requirements, however, Albrecht later commissioned Adolph Lohse, a pupil of the great Prussian architect Schinkel, to build another one in the Italian Renaissance style overlooking the vineyards. At the same time, the neighbouring Villa Stockhausen was built for the Prince's chamberlain. Acquired by a new owner, it came to be known as the Lingner Palace. Karl August Lingner was a manufacturer of a well-known brand of mouthwash and he also founded the city's Hygiene Museum. His will stipulated that the building should be given over to public use after his death. He was buried in the mausoleum – the work in 1916 of Hans Poelzig – that is located on the slopes of the vineyard. Unfortunately, the results of public ownership of the building appear not to be too promising at the moment. Jewel-like, the third of these notable villas atop the green Loschwitz Heights is Eckberg Palace, once also known as Villa Souchay. Sitting on a spur between Mordgrund and the Elbe, this sandstone villa was built from 1859–61 by Christian Friedrich Arnold for the English businessman John Daniel Souchay. Arnold, who trained under Schinkel, designed this villa in neo-gothic style, and it is regarded as his masterpiece. The gardens are uniquely suited to the villa in which a late romantic influence still lingers. Schloss Eckberg is now an exclusive hotel that welcomes guests of the German government.

Die drei Schlösser am Elbhang vom Blauen Wunder aus gesehen.
The three great villas on the Loschwitz Heights seen from the Blaues Wunder.

Blick von Schloss Eckberg am Elbhang zum Blauen Wunder.
Looking from Schloss Eckberg on the Loschwitz Heights towards the Blaues Wunder.

Loschwitz

Loschwitz

Der rechtselbische Stadtteil mit Resten eines alten Dorfkerns kam erst 1921 zu Dresden. Bis Mitte des 19. Jahrhunderts war die Ortsflur noch drei-geteilt: Die Ratsgemeinde lag um die Kirche, ein anderer Teil erstreckte sich im Loschwitzgrund (heute Grundstraße) bis hinauf nach Bühlau und die Winzergemeinde siedelte an den Hängen Richtung Wachwitz. Es muss ein geruhsamer Ort gewesen sein, der vor allem von Künstlern wie dem roman-tischen Maler Ludwig Richter gern besucht wurde. Friedrich Schiller dichtete im Weinberg seines Freundes Gottfried Körner – das »Schillerhäuschen« ist heute noch erhalten. Der Fotograf August Kotzsch hielt seit Mitte des 19. Jahrhunderts die einfachen Häuser in den Weinbergen und die Mühlen im Loschwitzgrund mit viele Liebe zum Detail fest. Aber auch der Bau des Blauen Wunders, das den Fährbetrieb zwischen Blasewitz und Loschwitz ablöste, wurde von ihm dokumentiert. Das Leonhardimuseum, die Villen auf dem Weißen Hirsch und das Künstlerhaus gegenüber dem Loschwitzer Friedhof erinnern daran, dass um 1900 hier ein nobler Stadtteil entstanden war. Zum Glück blieb Loschwitz von den Zerstörungen des 13. Februar 1945 verschont, nur die Kirche brannte bis auf die Grundmauern nieder. Der achteckige Zentralbau mit Dachreiter von George Bähr und Johann Christian Fehre entstand zwischen 1705 bis 1708 und gilt als Vorläufer der Frauenkirche. Anfang der neunziger Jahre konnte dank des Einsatzes einer Bürgerinitiative mit so prominenten Mitgliedern wie Theo Adam und Peter Schreier mit dem Wiederaufbau der Pfarrkirche begonnen werden. Als besonderes Kleinod birgt sie den prächtigen Renaissance-Altar von Nosse-ni, der aus der abgerissenen Sophienkirche am Postplatz stammt. Vom Charme der Gründerjahre erzählen die Wohn- und Geschäftshäuser am Körnerplatz, in deren Schatten sich die niedrigen Fachwerkhäuser ducken und urbane Entwicklung erlebbar machen.

The villa suburb of Loschwitz was independent until it became part of Dres-den in 1921. Even before then, it was popular with the city's upper classes who owned vineyards here as long ago as the fifteenth century. In the sev-enteenth century and later, this was where successful people wanted a sec-ond home, including chapel master Heinrich Schütz and the court jeweller Johann Melchior Dinglinger. It was a peaceful place that attracted artists and writers, among them the German Romantic painter Ludwig Richter and Friedrich Schiller, who wrote his play *Don Carlos* in the vineyard home of his sponsor, Gottfried Körner; the house can still be seen in Schillerstrasse. In the late nineteenth century, a local man, August Kotzsch, began photo-graphing the area's simple vineyard homes and mills; he also made a photo-graphic record of the construction of the Blaues Wunder (incidentally a German phrase for a surprise) that finally brought to an end the old ferry service between Blasewitz and Loschwitz. The Leonhardi Museum, the villas in Weisser Hirsch and the Artists' House opposite Loschwitz cemetery are reminders that by 1900 Loschwitz was seriously patrician. Thankfully it was spared on 13 February 1945; only its church was destroyed. An octagonal building with a mansard roof and spire, it was the work of George Bähr and Johann Christian Fehre from 1705–08 and was the forerunner of the Frauenkirche. Thanks to the efforts of campaigners, including the Meissen-born tenor and conductor Peter Schreier, the church was reconstructed in the early 1990s. It now houses Nosseni's magnificent 1606 altar that was rescued from the now demolished Sophienkirche on Dresden's Postplatz. The low half-timbered houses and the late nineteenth-century tenement buildings and shops overlooking them on Loschwitz's Körnerplatz are fine examples of urban development.

Die Loschwitzer Kirche.
Loschwitz Church.

Blick vom Blasewitzer Ufer auf den Loschwitzer Hang.
View from Blasewitz on to the Loschwitz slope.

Oben: Winzerhäuser an der Friedrich-Wieck-Straße.
Unten: Gründerzeitgebäude am Körnerplatz.
Top: Winegrowers' homes in Friedrich-Wieck-Strasse.
Bottom: Late nineteenth-century buildings on Körnerplatz.

Weinberge und Obstplantagen am Elbhang sowie ein ausgedehnter englischer Park, bekannt für seine dendrologischen Kostbarkeiten, säumen die anmutige Schlossanlange der barocken Sommerresidenz der Wettiner. Mit einer Freitreppe, von der die Hofgesellschaft vom Wasserpalais (1720/21), wie sein Ebenbild das Bergpalais eine Schöpfung Pöppelmanns, zu den Gondeln am sächsischen Canal Grande gelangte, betonte August der Starke sein Repräsentationsbedürfnis. Ebenso wie das Japanische Palais greifen beide Palais mit den konkav geschwungenen, über bemalte Hohlkehlen kragenden Dächern die damals vorherrschende chinesische Mode auf, die sich im Abbilden fernöstlicher Lebensweise – nach europäischen Vorstellungen – widerspiegelte. Augusts Nachfolger erweiterten durch Seitenflügel das Schloss. Anfang des 19. Jahrhunderts fügte Christian Traugott Weinling anstelle des abgebrannten Renaissanceschlosses das dreiflügelige Neue Palais mit dem Fliederhof hinzu, das hauptsächlich in der Innengestaltung der klassizistische Formensprache entsprach.

Die schlichte evangelische Weinbergskirche (Nomen est omen) mit dem hölzernen Dachreiter, ebenfalls nach Plänen Pöppelmanns entstanden, wurde dem König als Ersatz für die beim Schlossbau abgetragene spätgotische Kirche abgetrotzt. Die Sanierung des Bauwerks in den neunziger Jahren geht auf eine Bürgerinitiative zurück.

Viele Künstler wie Carl Maria von Weber oder Richard Wagner bewohnten im Sommer die malerischen Weingüter in Pillnitz und Umgebung.

Vineyards and orchards on the Elbe heights and an extensive park in the English style frame the elegant baroque palace at Pillnitz where the house of Wettin took up summer residence. Like its counterpart the Bergpalais (Hill Palace), the Wasserpalais (Water Palace) is largely Pöppelmann's work from 1720–21. Built with its entrance overlooking the river, it is fronted by a wide representative flight of steps leading to the waterside where gondolas on Saxony's very own Grand Canal awaited the royal party. The curved pagoda roofs, chimneys that look like lanterns and decorative Chinese scenes on the façade and curved mouldings (cavetti) are all expressions of the contemporary fashion for chinoiserie. Early in the nineteenth century, Christian Traugott Weinling added the three wings of the Neues Palais (New Palace) as a replacement for the old Renaissance palace that fire had reduced to ruins. With its Fliederhof, Weinling's addition, in particular the interior design, is neoclassical in style. Yet another of Pöppelmann's designs, the simple Protestant Weinbergskirche (vineyard church) with its wooden ridge turret had to be wrung from the king following the demolition of its precursor. In the 1990s, the building was refurbished thanks to the efforts of local campaigners. Numerous famous names, such as Carl Maria von Weber and Richard Wagner, used to spend the summer here on the picturesque wine-growing estates and in fishermen's homes.

Raddampfer vor dem Wasserpalais.
Paddle steamer in front of the Water Palace.

Die Weinbergskirche inmitten der Pillnitzer Rebenhänge.
Weinberg Church in its vineyard setting.

Der Lustgarten zwischen Wasser- und Bergpalais.
The formal gardens between the Wasserpalais and Bergpalais.

PIESCHEN

TRACHEN-
BERGE

DD-
Pieschen

ALBERT-
STADT

Flughafen
Dresden

S S-Bahn
H Straßenbahn
H Buslinie

D R

45

46

43

42

RADEBERGER

Messe
Dresden
15

AUSSERE
NEUSTADT

NEUSTADT

VORSTADT

39

Alberthafen 12

DD-Neustadt

FRIEDRICH-

13

40

14

DD-Mitte

41

11

10

Johannstadt

STADT

1

2

3 6
5
9
8 7
4
16

17

28

21
18 20
19

22

27

26

Grosser

SÜD
VORSTADT
WEST

Zoologischer
Garten

Garten

DD-Hauptbahnhof

24

PLAUEN

SÜD
VORSTADT
OST

25

DD-Strehlen

23

STREHLEN